The
NEW ENGLAND
COMPANION

The
NEW ENGLAND
COMPANION

Naomi Black and Mary Forsell

MALLARD
PRESS

MALLARD PRESS
An imprint of BDD Promotional Book Company, Inc.
666 Fifth Avenue New York, New York 10103

A TERN ENTERPRISE BOOK

Published by MALLARD PRESS
An imprint of BDD Promotional Book Company, Inc.
666 Fifth Avenue
New York, New York 10103

Mallard Press and its accompanying design and logo are trademarks of BDD Promotional Book Company, Inc.

ISBN 0-792-45308-5

THE NEW ENGLAND COMPANION
was prepared and produced by
Tern Enterprise
15 West 26th Street
New York, NY 10010

Editor: Stephen Williams
Designer: Judy Morgan
Photography Editor: Ede Rothaus

ADDITIONAL PHOTOGRAPHY: 34, 39, 43a,b Society for the Preservation of New England Antiquities, photographs © J. David Bohl; 46a © Ulf Sjostedt/FPG International; 46b © Lynn Karlin; 47a,b Shelburne Museum, Shelburne, Vermont; 90 Courtesy of Four Winds Craft Guild, Nantucket, photograph © Jack Weinhold; 107, 108 Courtesy of the Sandwich Historical Society/Glass Museum

Illustrations by Judy L. Morgan

Typeset by: The Interface Group, Inc.
Color Separations by: Scantrans Pte. Ltd.
Printed and bound in Singapore by Tien Wah Press (PTE) Limited

Acknowledgments

The following people have graciously offered their recipes and recollections for use or adaptation in this book. We wish to thank Marlyn Flanders, Flanders' Bean-Hole-Beans Co., Epsom, New Hampshire; Kenyon Corn Meal Co., Usquepaugh, Rhode Island; David Marvin, Butternut Mountain Farm, Johnson, Vermont; Tim McTague, Gray's Grist Mill, Adamsville, Rhode Island; Harry Morse, Morse Farm Sugar Shack, Montpelier, Vermont; Warren Picower, managing editor, Food and Wine magazine, New York City; The Vermont Country Store, Weston, Vermont; Jackie La Bella, The Connecticut Valley Tourism Commission, Middletown Connecticut.

Thanks should also go to Carol Griffin, of the Yankee Candle Co., South Deerfield, Massachusetts; scrimshander David Lazarus, Nantucket, Massachusetts; Carol Leveque, of the Vermont Chamber of Commerce; Lauren Maxwell, of the State of Maine Department of Marine Resources; research librarian Carolyn Freeman Travers, of Plimouth Plantation, Plymouth, Massachusetts; basketmaker and author Martha Weatherbee, Sanbornton, New Hampshire; the Nantucket Historical Society.

And finally we want to acknowledge our skilled editor Stephen Williams, and designer Judy Morgan.

CONTENTS

The incredible diversity, history, natural beauty and lore of New England cannot easily be contained in one book, but we've done our best to give you a good sample. The New England Companion *paints a broad portrait of this distinctive American region and guides the reader to experiencing its best assets.*

Within these pages, the range of historic New England tradition is presented in such a way that the contemporary reader with a passion for the architectural and interior home styles, collectibles, crafts, gardens, food and entertaining styles of the past can update them for the present. Throughout this book are innovative ideas from contemporary practitioners of New England traditions—people whose work bespeaks the Yankee style and spirit and who appreciate the richness of the past and use it as a starting point for their own work.

This book tells you about the traditional designs for colonial homes, and offers ideas on how to reinterpret these motifs in modern homes. And to help infuse your home's interior with a New England feel, we offer you photos and information about the most coveted pottery, glassware, and other New England collectibles. There are even some

instructions for traditional crafts you can make—with centuries-old handiwork methods updated to use more modern materials and techniques. The grounds surrounding New England homes also represent the unique Yankee spirit, and The New England Companion *examines the range of New England garden styles. Much of what is now called American cooking descends directly from traditional New England foods. The* New England Companion *delves into the hearty dishes that have emerged from New England, many of them influenced by Native American practices, and provides a recipe sampler so you can try a variety of dishes. Finally, there is the section called Sources, where you learn how to locate wonderful New England-originated designs; historic New England locales; and museums and other places where you can view authentic New England homes and gardens as well as crafts and collectibles. Using this section as a point of reference for experiencing this rugged region "hands-on" makes it possible to move on to discover your own, personal New England.*

We hope you have a wonderful journey.

—Naomi Black and Mary Forsell

NEW ENGLAND HOMES & INTERIORS

The homes of New England and their furnishings convey the diversity of this region, and their designs directly reflect the progression of history. Their persistence is a tangible measure of the success and continued viability of many old New England architectural and interior design styles.

Such indigenous New England building materials as shingles and clapboard are still used today, and they function just as well as they did in previous centuries. The basic form of the saltbox house is as viable now as it was in Colonial times, because it easily sheds snow and has a versatile interior space. The current

ubiquitousness of the Cape Cod style of the Colonial era is testimony to the basic soundness of its design.

Similarly, in New England interiors, styles and motifs have kept pace with life-styles. The hearth has always been a symbol of New England, but in recent decades it has been combined with such features as high ceilings and floor-to-ceiling windows from which to view the stunning landscape, whether it is the rugged coastline or a quiet fir forest. And the furniture fashioned by craftsmen centuries ago has also influenced many of today's designs and reflects a regional sensibility in the use of native woods, such as ash and maple.

*L*angdon House in *Portsmouth, New Hampshire, reflects the grand architectural sensibilities of the Georgian era in its balustraded portico, dormer windows, and Corinthian corner pilasters (page 10). A contemporary New England home features large windows to view the outdoors (page 12). Also in harmony with its environment, Betsey Ross House in Nantucket echoes the blue-gray color of the Atlantic (this page, top). The hearth is the quintessential symbol of the New England homestead (this page, bottom).*

© Robert Perron

13

Architecture

Despite the fact that New England homes are now famous for their finely crafted details, stylized architecture was hardly a priority for the first colonists arriving in the New World in the early seventeenth century. But protection from the elements was, and the colonists quickly erected simple dwellings to serve their basic needs.

The very first buildings were simple wigwam-style houses, and not, as popular belief would have it, log cabins. These houses were hybrids of two basic styles: the many serviceable native Algonquian dwellings that dotted the New England coastline and the huts of shepherds, woodsmen, and charcoal burners of the settlers' native England. The wigwam-hut homes, fashioned from poles, branches, and rushes and held together by clay, were distinguished from the Native American dwellings by wood-frame doorways and clay-lined chimneys. In some cases, the colonists even created primitive dugout dwellings in the sides of hills. However, these were all temporary measures.

© Robert Perron

The Colonial Styles

Before long, the colonists were erecting more traditional-looking structures. These first early homes consisted of only one large room and were called Great Houses. Bunks were set up within the room, and entire families lived in them. The colonists also began to build wooden cottages, drawing on English regional styles. These too were one-room structures and were characterized by a few small casement windows, thatch roofs, a steep roofline, and a large masonry fireplace against one wall.

To afford additional space, sleeping lofts were built within the house, accessible by way of narrow stairs abutting the chimney. Interior and exterior ornamentation were minimal,

and materials were used in the most straightforward manner possible. Another modification to the harsh New England climate was the orientation of the house to a southern exposure to capture all available warmth.

But even this design proved inadequate for their needs. Thatch in England shed rainwater and stayed put; in the less hospitable environment of the New World, it often blew right off the house. And so the colonists began to use a local material, slate. The exposed frame, or Tudor-style exterior worked well in England, but in the New England climate it expanded and contracted as a result of dramatic weather changes. So, wooden frames

It was a queer sort of place—a gable-ended old house, one side palsied as it were, and leaning over sadly. It stood on a sharp bleak corner.... Entering that gable-ended Spouter-Inn, you found yourself in a wide, low, straggling entry with old-fashioned wainscots, reminding one of the bulwarks of some condemned old craft.
—Herman Melville
Moby Dick; or,
The Whale

14

_A_ weathered colonial home in historic Deerfield, Massachusetts, located in the Connecticut River Valley, is equipped with an overhang roof for protection from wind, rain, and snow (top). Small casement windows precisely fitted with diamond-shaped panes of glass are another typical Colonial feature (bottom). They are pictured at Hoxie House, a saltbox-style home built in the Cape Cod town of Sandwich in 1637.

© Robert Perron

*T*he massive form of the Old Ship Meetinghouse in Hingham, Massachusetts, conveys a quiet power. Its basic geometric shape, unfussy white color, modest-size windows, and lack of ornamentation—save for the requisite steeple—are hallmarks of the Puritan sense of order and simplicity.

© Paul E. Johnson/Decisive Moment

of the homes were sheathed with split clapboard made from locally abundant larch and oak. By 1633, "clapboard ryvers" were doing such a thriving business milling the larch and oak in the Massachusetts Bay Colony that the colony began regulating their wages.

As would be expected, as families grew and the colonists got their feet on the ground, the need for more space in their homes became pressing and in the mid-seventeenth century rooms began to be added on. Houses were sometimes modified by putting a large two-sided fireplace in the center of the house and flanking it with two separate rooms. A central entryway with a petite foyer allowed access to either of the ground-floor rooms. Exposed beams, called summers, supported space on the second floor. All rooms were of an intimate size, despite the apparent massiveness of such homes from the outside, for the framing elements of the house took up much of the interior space. Fortunately, the colonists were generally smaller than people today, and simply didn't need a lot of space. They also wanted to limit the amount of space that needed to be heated. Other features of such homes were an upper floor that extended beyond the lower floor on the exterior of the house, called an overhang. This architectural device sheltered the house.

Adjoining rooms were also often added by way of the lean-to—a structural addition to the back of the house that continued but did not adjoin the roof line. Initially, these lean-tos were slightly sunken and did not reach the top of the first story. However, as time passed, homes' fronts were built a half-story higher and lean-tos were built one story high; the resulting steep roof connecting the main house with the lean-to was called a saltbox. The southeastern part of the lean-to at this point might have acted as an extra bedroom, often called a borning room because it was where childbirth took place. The other half of the addition might house a kitchen, in which case the chimney would have to have been enlarged to extend to the back of the house. The northeast corner of the addition was usually made into a "buttery," a cool room for storing food. Extant examples of saltbox homes include the Connecticut landmarks Old Ogden House, in Fairfield, and the Samuel Whitman house, in Farmington, as well as Vermont's Dutton House, at the Shelburne Museum.

Another New England–specific style was the garrison house, built principally to shelter townspeople from attacks by Native Americans. The garrison house was usually built on the edge of a town or territory. This style was most prevalent during the mid-seventeenth century, when tensions with Native American tribes were at their greatest, but continued to be built up until the mid-eighteenth century. Garrison homes were characterized by heavy timber and small, portholelike windows with shutters that opened for a lookout. In the two-story garrisons, the second story overhung the first for added protection. Towns erected brick garrisons whenever feasible because they couldn't be burned down. In most cases, old garrison houses were

They passed through two or three small, short streets, which, with their little wooden houses, with still more wooden dooryards, looked as if they had been constructed by the nearest carpenter and his boy—a sightless, soundless, interspaced, embryonic region....
—Henry James
The Bostonians

remodeled in the eighteenth century, with larger windows installed, and the examples still standing do not have their original appearance. You can find examples of these houses throughout New England. In Massachusetts, there is the Nathaniel Peaslee Garrison House, in West Newbury, and the Hazzen-Spiller Garrison House, in Haverhill. In Maine, the Major Charles Frost Garrison House, in East Eliot, and the McIntire Garrison House, in Scotland, near York, are still standing.

By 1654, the writer Edward Johnson was able to observe in his book, *Wonder-Working Providence of Sions Savior in New-England*: "The Lord hath been pleased to turn all the wigwams, huts, and hovels the English dwelt in at their first coming, into orderly, fair, and well-built houses,

well furnished many of them...."

From here, Colonial architecture became more inventive, as different homes were designed to appeal to individual tastes. To increase second-floor living space, the roofline of the Colonial home was expanded. The result was the gambrel roof, which sloped gently from two sides at the top and then became steeper. This form was sometimes combined with the beloved saltbox roof. The Cape Cod home (well-known even today to suburban dwellers across America because of mass reproduction in the suburban building boom in the mid-twentieth century) also developed in various manifestations. An original resident of Cape Cod, where its low stature made it a cozy dwelling among harsh seaside winds, this house style

Yankee mariners and foreign seamen have long looked to the New England lighthouse to guide them past the hazards of the rocky coastline (left). The meetinghouse is another indigenous New England form (right). This one, in Washington, New Hampshire, displays all the traditional hallmarks: clapboard exterior, open belfry, and a tower topped with a weathervane. Meetinghouses were usually sited on high ground facing the village green.

19

took several forms. The half Cape consisted of five rooms, three on the first floor and two on the second. The door was located to one side of the front of the house. With the three-quarter Cape, another room was added to the first floor, and the door position shifted toward the center of the front of the house, although it was still an asymmetrical orientation. The full Cape is the model of symmetry and is perhaps the quintessential American dream home. The front door was located in the center of the home, flanked by two sets of two windows, and the interior of the home was expanded accordingly, making it into a commodious dwelling with as many as eight rooms. Although still covered with clapboard, as with the earliest cottages, these homes were sheathed

with smooth white pine, and mortar and bricks had superseded hay, clay and and other makeshift materials. On the inside, plaster was used to cover beams as well as the walls.

Throughout New England, wonderful, quirky variations arose in home styles. In the same tradition as the lean-to add-on, houses became personalized to accommodate the tastes of their owners. Individual homes evolved over time as such architectural features as gables, dormers, ells, wings, and sheds were added when the homes changed owners. Examples include the Massachusetts landmarks the Old Iron Master's House, in Saugus, which boasts steep gables and an overhang, and the John Whipple House in Ipswich, with a steep-pitched roof and lean-to addition.

The Georgian Home

New Englanders were becoming status conscious as the colonies' wealth grew in the beginning of the eighteenth century. Naturally, architecture reflected this and homes became even more sophisticated. Although the word *Georgian* is generally applied to buildings of the early eighteenth century because of the Georges reigning in England, the architecture in America is distinct from Old World buildings.

Architecture took on a less severe air than the early Colonial architecture had possessed. American dwellings became more balanced and ornamented during the period from approximately 1735 to 1790. More refined details began to be added to the exteriors and interiors of the homes. Roof lines were no longer steeply pitched, and the gently sloping mansard roof emerged. Ornate chimneys became a hallmark of the Georgian period. Cornices and molding all became decorative features of the exterior of the home. If a roof was double-hipped, it was likely to sport showy dormer windows, a third story, and even a decorative fence surrounding the rooftop. Rooftops might also have captain's and widow's walks.

For more modest homes, clapboard continued to be a popular feature, but it was apt to be painted in refined pastel tones, such as yellow or salmon. More affluent New Englanders, particularly those living in Boston or Newport, opted for brickwork in delicate reddish shades. The size of the home was greatly expanded, not only by the third story added by the double-hipped roof, but in depth as well. Fireplaces were no longer grouped together in the center of the house, but were located at ends of the house. Doorways became the focus of great architectural ornamentation, often topped by windows, friezes, pediments set on pilasters, and other classical motifs. They became symbols of the status of the family and actually took on symbolic significance that varied by region. In Newport, Rhode Island, the broken pediment over a doorway might frame a carved pineapple, which was the symbol of hospitality. While in Deerfield, Massachusetts, the stately swan pediment was common, representing prestige.

In Maine, the Sarah Orne Jewett House in South Berwick and Hamilton House in Berwick are fine extant examples of the Georgian style. In Massachusetts, the Codman House in Lincoln, and the Jeremiah Lee Mansion in Marblehead also embody Georgian architectural principles.

A white picket fence neatly surrounds the Sarah Orne Jewett home in South Berwick, Maine (top). Jewett lived in this elaborate Georgian home for much of her life, to write stories and novels. The residence is particularly distinguished by its beautifully preserved interior (bottom). The entry hall is graced by an exquisitely carved staircase and fine woodwork.

Society for the Preservation of New England Antiquities/ photograph © J. David Bohl

Society for the Preservation of New England Antiquities/ photograph © J. David Bohl

21

The Federal Style

The Federal period in architecture (1790–1820) was the natural successor to the Georgian period characterized by a more delicate design and lightness. Despite its distinct American look, Federal architecture's genesis was in Europe. The early eighteenth-century discovery of the ancient Italian cities of Pompeii and Herculaneum, which were buried in the first century A.D. by the eruption of Mount Vesuvius, eventually became fuel for the neoclassical design vocabulary, which manifested itself in different forms in the Old World. In the United States, the fervor for antiquity emerged as the Federal style. The Constitution had been adopted in 1788, and there was a great surge in national pride. Borrowing from the design vocabulary of classical antiquity, homes were designed with attention paid to proportion and balance. The Federal style interpreted the preceding Georgian style and made it even more refined. Exterior ornamentation became more attenuated and linear. A refined balustrade might run around the roof, encircling the thin, elegant chimneys, particularly in the townhouses of Boston. Architecture as a symbol of the country's strength was emphasized more than ever. This belief was especially asserted in Asher Benjamin's book, *The American Builder's Companion: or a New System of Architecture Particularly Adapted to the Present Style of Building in the United States of America*, which was published in Boston in 1806.

Federal architecture was, more than any type that preceded it, a style for the wealthy, and it became manifest in Salem, Massachusetts, whose rise as a shipping port resulted in a wealthy populace. It was here that Samuel McIntire (1757–1811) was born and lived. Trained as a woodcarver, McIntire applied this skill to his architecture, which is amply represented in Salem. His eminently American homes exude an unpretentious, gracious yet refined spirit. McIntire's finest work is considered to be the John Gardner-Pinigree House; this building has come to represent the height of the neoclassical Federalist style in America. Built in 1805, this refined home boasts a doorway flanked by Corinthian columns with the portico carved in wood to look like stone. The house stands three stories tall and is topped by a balustraded parapet. Made of brick, it is ornamented by subtle strips of marble marking each story. The interior of this and other Federalist homes built in Salem possessed the same refined qualities. Such Federalist buildings stand in sharp contrast to that other famous home of Salem, the House of Seven Gables, which is an excellent representation of the seventeenth-century New England home, with its steep roof, second-floor overhang, and weathered clapboards. Other classic Federal houses still standing are the Nickels-Sortwell House in Wiscasset, Maine, the Harrison Gray Otis House, in Boston's Beacon Hill section (designed by the Boston-bred, Harvard-educated architect Charles Bulfinch, who sought to make Boston a rival of any European city), and Merwin House in Stockbridge, Massachusetts.

In 1807, Captain William Nickels undertook construction of a new house in Wiscasset, Maine. The retired master mariner wanted the residence to reflect his high stature in the community with regal form, generous windows, and a carved colonnade. Today, the stunning Federal mansion draws visitors from all over to admire the lofty facade (page 23).

Society for the Preservation of New England Antiquities/
photograph © J. David Bohl

Greek Revival

The Greek Revival emphasized stately architectural elements of the Old World and made them look right at home in America. Neoclassicism is clearly at play in the Ionic columns and crisp monumental form of this temple-style Maine building (page 25).

Greek Revival, a style popular in America in the years 1815–1860, was a natural extension of Federal architecture. It still drew on classical motifs but allowed them to stand largely unadorned, beautiful in their simplicity. Although this style was known throughout the United States, in New England it was realized in such Boston structures as the Sears House (built in 1815) and the Quincy Market (1825), both designed by the architect Alexander Parris. The buildings have minimal ornament, and their austere style and interplay of columns and granite—meant to resemble marble— betray a Grecian reference point. The style also found expression throughout New England, in homes such as the Charles Clapp House in Portland, Maine, and even at miscellaneous farmhouses, where local carpenters freely interpreted the Greek orders.

The nineteenth century was an era filled with a variety of architecture styles, some of which influenced New England, others of which found their truest expression elsewhere in America. Among these styles were Queen Anne, Gothic Revival, and Italianate. Toward the end of the Victorian era, a style geared to summer living in New England emerged. Dubbed the shingle style because of its use of shingles that could range in color from rich red to green and natural brown, it was sometimes combined with clapboard, but more often than not it was shingles that completely sheathed the house.

The result was meant to have a relaxed, casual look associated with country living. Spacious, wraparound porches and balconies were widely incorporated into such homes because of their summertime associations. Stone masonry, massed in boulder forma- tions, might line the foundation of the house. The roofs of such homes might include gables, a reference to New England's Colonial past, as the Victorian era was the age of revivals. Examples of the shingle style are plentiful throughout New England, particularly along the seaboard. Among such buildings are the architectural firm of McKim, Mead & White's Newport Casino and the Isaac Bell House, both in Newport, Rhode Island.

The twentieth century has seen an even greater return to the styles of New England's past. Today, many homes are built in the saltbox and Cape Cod styles, often greatly expanded to make the homes more commodious. Others are starker contemporary dwellings that allude to the past in clever architectural "puns." Such an example is the Gropius House in Lincoln, Massachusetts. Erected in 1938 by the architect Walter Gropius, the home has traditional white-painted New England clapboard on its interior, rather than sheathing its exterior. The clapboard is oriented vertically instead of horizontally. There are numerous architects working in New England today who draw upon the styles of the past but adapt them to contemporary New England life-styles.

Reading Really Sticks to You.

THE BUBBLE GU[...]
BOOKSTO[...]
48 Main Street [...]
Sutter Cree[...] (20[...]

© Brian Vanden Brink

HOMES AND INTERIORS

THE HOUSE OF SEVEN GABLES

One famous house in Salem, Massachusetts, was designed in part to protect a family from witch hunters. Traditionally, witches were held responsible for all maleficence in society, and around 1692 in Salem, there certainly seemed to be evil in the air: The French and Indian Wars were raging; British taxes were exorbitant; squabbles among villagers over land ownership abounded; smallpox was prevalent.

The Salem witchhunt was initiated by a group of young women who regularly visited the home of the Reverend Samuel Parris to hear his West Indian slave Tituba tell them demonic tales of the islands. Two of the girls, aged nine and eleven, were so affected by the folklore that they would sob violently at the gatherings. Seeing that their behaviour was pardoned, they also indulged in these hysterical fits at home. Their outbursts inspired the other girls—who ranged in age from fifteen to twenty—to do the same, and it became an adolescent prank to act up and blame it on specters that were haunting and taunting them. When asked who was torturing them, they at first pointed to the most powerless people in Salem: a beggar woman, a woman with an illegitimate son, and even Tituba herself.

Soon, the young women began to expand upon their circle of suspects until not even the wealthiest landowners were spared, including Mrs. Philip English, who lived in a stately home in Salem. Mrs. English's residence was just a five-minute walk from the famous House of Seven Gables, then known as the Turner Mansion, for the family who lived there. John Turner II, a young man who, because of the death of both parents, was responsible for his sisters' welfare, must have been frightened by the hysteria.

In The Chronicles of Three Old Houses, *Caroline O. Emmerton speculates that John Turner II, having witnessed the fate of Mrs. English, would have been anxious to protect his sisters in the event that any of them were accused of witchcraft. One of the features of the House of Seven Gables is a secret staircase, which has led to much speculation. Emmerton writes, "Can there be any doubt that he began to plan to protect them, and whatever plan he hit upon a temporary hiding place in the house would probably be needed. I believe that he built the secret staircase for that purpose...."*

More than a century later, when Nathaniel Hawthorne wrote House of Seven Gables *(1851), he drew upon his knowledge of the witchcraft hysteria from his cousin, Susannah Ingersoll, whose family had bought the house from the Turners in 1686.*

Courtesy of the House of Seven Gables Settlement Association

*Half-way down a by-street of one of our New England towns stands a rusty wooden house, with seven acutely peaked gables, facing towards various points of the compass, and a huge, clustered chimney in the midst.... The aspect of the venerable mansion has always affected me like a human countenance bearing the traces not merely of outward storm and sunshine, but expressive, also, of the long lapse of mortal life, and accompanying vicissitudes that have passed within.
—Nathaniel Hawthorne* The House of the Seven Gables *(1851)*

Architect Robert W. Knight designs homes with an eye to their surroundings. For this one in Deer Isle, Maine, skylights and oversize windows distribute natural light throughout the house while also providing views of the landscape and sky above. The terrace also serves to connect the house with the outdoors. An icy outdoor winter scene contrasts with the warmth of interior woodwork in another home designed by Knight (page 29).

The Contemporary New England Architect

In one respect, the challenge for the New England architect practicing today has not changed a great deal since the colonists first began building homes in the wilderness of the New World: designing a building that stands up to the harsh, changeable weather. But now people insist that homes fit their aesthetic sense as well.

Robert W. Knight practices architecture in Blue Hill, Maine, and points out that because the contemporary New England architect must confront the same weather conditions as those faced by the colonists, the resulting architecture bears a similarity to original New England buildings. He says, "This is an area that traditionally builds frame houses that are clad in wood. The weather is hard on masonry, because

on the coast there's a lot of freeze-and-frost cycles. The impact of the weather here on buildings is tremendous, and you must recognize the factors of long winters and dark skies on the inhabitants."

Of course, contemporary New Englanders do not have the same lifestyles as their forebears, and architects also have to allow for this difference in their designs. In the seventeenth century, colonists sought shelter from harsh, driving winds and deliberately kept windows small to conserve heat as well as provide protection from attacks by Native Americans. Knight says, "I think the big difference between now and one hundred years ago is that back then people usually made their living outside and when they returned home

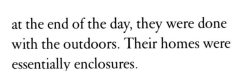

at the end of the day, they were done with the outdoors. Their homes were essentially enclosures.

"Nowadays, more people work indoors, so they want their house to be a bridge to the outdoors, and appreciate features such as oversized vistas of glass overlooking the sea. We now have better technology for that. The houses we do are pieces from New England forms, but they certainly have much more glass and the orientation is different. And we use traditional elements such as porches as bridges to the outside."

Within the context of New England, there are a variety of natural environments that call for different architectural styles and reflect a sense of place. Knight purports, "Of all the factors that go into house design, the site is unquestionably the most important one in terms of the image of the house and the form of the house." In the same way that carpenters freely interpreted Greek Revival styles and built farmhouses with individualistic details meant to rivet the eye to the house, Knight designs houses in flat spaces so that they make a strong visual impact: "When we build houses in open fields, we echo that sense, designing an object that can sit freestanding." And this criterion changes with the site: "When you're building in a spruce forest, you face different kinds of requirements. The house becomes an object that wants to blend in with the land. It's less driven by the New England vernacular because it is not going to be seen as a separate entity."

© Robert Perron

In my native town of Salem…stands a spacious edifice of brick…. Its front is ornamented with a portico of half a dozen wooden pillars supporting a balcony, beneath which a flight of wide granite steps descends toward the street. Over the entrance hovers an enormous specimen of the American eagle, with outspread wings, a shield before her breast, and, if I recollect aright, a bunch of intermingled thunderbolts and barbed arrows in each claw.
—*Nathaniel Hawthorne* The Scarlet Letter

Because his firm is located near the Maine coast, most of the homes Knight designs are on or near the water. While he executes oceanfront homes in a variety of forms, he is always conscious of the traditional styles of the past used on the waterfront—such as Cape Cod and shingle style—and seeks to have his contemporary structures harmonize with their surroundings. "Whatever we do doesn't have to look like the other buildings—but it should be speaking in the same language. It ought to look like an evolution."

Variations on the shingle style are a personal favorite for Knight. In open, windswept sites, he may choose to build low, roof-dominated shingle style homes; a site with an abundance of trees may call for a taller structure to afford views. Knight feels particularly enthusiastic about shingles for their utility and beauty: "The shingled wall is probably the most weathertight of all and, nicely enough, the least expensive. It also doesn't require maintenance and just needs to be reshingled every twenty-five or thirty years." Depending on the

environment they are exposed to, the shingles react differently over time: they become a silvery gray when exposed to sun and saltwater; used inland, they turn a darker gray. Knight prefers to leave shingles unpainted on coastal homes and give them a stain inland.

In the nineteenth century, the shingle style house was popular as a summer residence, and the style was more flamboyant than other New England forms. "In those days, people were willing for a summer house to take on a more radical architectural form than their primary residences. And I think that's still true with my clients who are summer people—who have a house elsewhere. They want to try something different. They want to live their secret life here."

Another thing that hasn't changed much from New England's past is an emphasis on old-fashioned workmanship. To carry out his designs, Knight draws on a body of local builders and craftspeople who bring a sense of pride to their work, which he feels is unusual compared to other regions. He feels that this is because "the builders are Yankees at heart."

Knight usually does not advise his clients on how their homes should be furnished unless they specifically ask for an opinion, but does feel strongly that the interior and exterior aspects of a home should not compete. This does not mean that elements of old and new can't be combined, but they should be mixed with some forethought. Colonial architecture—which has a severity and angularity about it—works well with a somewhat stark contemporary interior. Similarly, Knight feels, a flamboyant Victorian exterior does not mix well with a restrained interior. Above all, in terms of site and the building's interior, Knight says, "I like the house to be comfortable with itself."

*A*n outdoor walkway joins separate wings of a Knight-designed Maine home (page 30). This transitional space also provides a frame for a water view. Shingles were left unpainted to weather naturally (top). Local stone was a logical and durable choice to create a wall in the backyard (bottom).

© Robert Perron

© Robert Perron

Hallmarks of New England Architecture:

As America became more prosperous, the newfound wealth was reflected in its architectural details. The doorway in particular was emphasized and often embellished with decorative carving (this page, top and bottom). Steeply pitched gables bordered by decorative woodwork bring a craftsman quality to this residence on Block Island, Rhode Island (page 33).

Clapboard

Made from local woods such as split oak and white pine, clapboard is laid horizontally on the sides of homes to insulate them from the cold and to give them a finished look. It is still popular in the region today.

Elaborate doorways

In the Georgian period—particularly in the Connecticut River Valley and in Newport, Rhode Island—doorways received considerable design emphasis. Over doorways, fanlights, friezes, transoms, and pediments were common; flanking doorways, pilasters and shutters were often featured.

© Melabee Miller/Envision

Gables

The term gable refers to the triangularly shaped section that juts out from the end of a steeply pitched roof. It is most prominent when two gables facing different directions abut one another. This feature is common to seventeenth-century New England homes.

Overhangs and decorative drops

Common features of the late-seventeenth-century New England home were sculptural wooden carvings suspended from the four corners of the overhang—the second story of the house, which extended over the first to provide protection from the elements.

Window pediments

By the eighteenth century, New Englanders were also ornamenting their windows with pediments in a variety of shapes: swan necks, arches, and triangles were popular.

INTERIORS

New England furnishings are well known for fine craftsmanship. They have an enduring beauty and evoke the individualistic spirit of the region. Through studying the evolution of New England interiors, it's possible to trace the development of the region—from the first, rudimentary rooms of the early Colonial period to the lavishly decorated Federal parlors that reflected the optimism of a new nation.

In New England more than any other part of the United States, styles transmitted from abroad were interpreted more conservatively, and regional characteristics were stubbornly and consistently injected into the furniture forms. The earliest Colonial craftsmen were selective in their designs. Although they worked from Old World models, American furniture makers tended to freely select and combine decorative motifs. On the whole the Yankee artisans reinterpreted Continental designs in their own fashion—streamlining fussy motifs and focusing on creating sturdy, well-made, yet quickly executed, pieces of furniture.

In Colonial times, American craftsmen generally fell into three categories: the joiner, who constructed furniture with mortise-and-tendon joints; the turner, whose skill lay in creating furniture from turning wood on a lathe; and the cabinetmaker, who was considered a master craftsman, skilled in constructing and carving furniture. The joiners and turners tended to produce furniture through specialization and division of labor. The furniture was made in quantity and stockpiled. The cabinetmaker created more elaborate, made-to-order pieces.

Furniture created by all of these artisans exists today and has historical value for different reasons. The joiners and turners were more likely to create furniture with a vernacular stamp, because they were more at liberty to turn out designs for the general public, without adherence to European models. The master craftsman was more interested in realizing his client's dreams of what their furnishings should look like, usually based on European prototypes. The American style did not really come into its own until the eighteenth century, with the introduction of the William and Mary style.

Still, despite getting inspiration from Old World models, American furniture was never strictly derivative of European styles, for a number of reasons. Aside from the Yankee craftsman's tendency to simplify European designs, it must also be taken into account that in the seventeenth century, communication was slow and journeys were rigorous, so there was not the rapid interchange of information that we know today.

© Robert Perron

A Colonial chest of drawers displays hallmarks of the William and Mary era (page 34). During this time—the first quarter of the eighteenth century—hardware began to be imported to the Colonies, and brass plates and drawer pulls were first used on furniture. The hearth was essential to every Colonial home, and it was not unusual to find a Windsor chair set before it (this page). Windsor designs actually originated in England, but like so many other furniture forms were adapted into vernacular colonial forms. Connecticut was a major producer of Windsor hoopback chairs and settees.

Prentis House, a saltbox home originally built in 1733 in Hadley, Massachusetts—but now on display at the Shelburne Museum in Vermont—is filled with furnishings appropriate to the period. A William and Mary gate-leg table with turned supports and drop leaves looks quite at home with furniture and objects from the same era: a candlestand, wing chair with flame-stitched upholstery, and fine brass accessories.

Seventeenth-Century Styles

While the earliest furniture of the colonies (made between 1640 and 1710) has been referred to as "Pilgrim" or "Jacobean," no universally accepted stylistic term exists. Expert consensus favors the all-encompassing term *seventeenth-century*, but Early American furniture can also be referred to as "Colonial," because it runs parallel to what is basically called Colonial architecture.

The earliest Colonial furniture—most of which began to be produced in earnest after 1650—betrays its makers' ethnic origins. From their workshops in Ipswich, Massachusetts, Thomas Denis and William Searle created chests with elaborate carvings that echoed a style prevalent in their birthplace, the West Country of England. Thomas Mulliner's shop in New Haven, Connecticut, produced chests with arcaded panels—a Renaissance motif of English furniture. On the other hand, the furniture maker Peter Blin of Wethersfield, Connecticut, produced distinctly American chests subtly adorned with spindle shapes and carved with a distinctively New World plant: the sunflower. Another early American regionalism was the Carver Chair of New England, a turned armchair named for John Carver, the first governor of the Plymouth Colony. Carver Chairs were characterized by an interplay of thick back supports and thinner spindles used as auxiliary support throughout the chair. As in England, oak was a popular wood for such furniture in the colonies, although

Shelburne Museum, Shelburne, Vermont

A miniature cupboard displays humble treasures. Colonial New England families traditionally designed their cupboards so that they would fit exactly into corners, but there were also models that could be placed into recessed paneled walls.

© Robert Perron

native ash and maple were also used. There is evidence that much of the furniture was actually painted. Aside from paneling and carving, another popular form of ornamentation was ebonizing, or painting black, any ornamentation on the furniture.

The most popular and essential piece of Colonial furniture was undoubtedly the cupboard—used both to store household items such as linen and to display dishware. The chest was also essential for storage. Another popular piece of furniture was the trestle table, whose surface rested on X-shaped supports or stanchions. It resembled a giant picnic table, but usually had a detachable top so that it could be stored upright when not in use.

These very practical forms of furniture are indicative of the basic, rugged life-style of the New England colonists. The typical Colonial room was quite spartan, the walls lined with rough plaster or unfinished boards laid vertically. Furniture was minimal, but it tended to be so massive that the few pieces used would dominate a room.

The William and Mary Style

In contrast to the brass-tacks basics of seventeenth-century furnishings, the William and Mary style—which dates to the years 1700 to 1725—exploded in a profusion of ornament and actually gave rise to new types of furniture. This style derived from design currents in Europe, yet American craftsmen greatly simplified the baroque fussiness of the European models.

No longer did furniture have to serve some essential purpose to be admitted into the Colonial home. As with the concurrent Georgian style in architecture, homes were designed as much for beauty as for utility. The easy chair, highback armchair, daybed, gateleg table, highboy chest, butterfly leg table, and desk were all amenities of the William and Mary style. This mode of design stressed elaborate carvings (such as the "Spanish foot," a scroll form on the base of tables and chairs), meant to convey a sense of richness and opulence, carried out on walnut and maple furniture. Surface treatments such as walnut-burl veneers, japanning, and painted decoration added an extra visual dimension, and delicate dovetail construction resulted in lighter-looking furniture—which must have been a breath of fresh air compared to the medieval-looking early Colonial designs. Such flourishes as teardrop-shaped drawer pulls and shiny brass key plates made the furniture even more sophisticated. Room walls were no longer covered in rough wood or plaster but rather, were paneled to achieve a refined effect in keeping with the high-style furniture.

In the mid-eighteenth century, trade with China inspired objects and furniture with an Eastern air. This japanned highchest was designed in Boston sometime between 1733 and 1745 and simulates the look of Oriental lacquer.

Queen Anne and Chippendale Styles

For every style or movement, a backlash always seems to ensue. The Queen Anne style, the successor to William and Mary, was a reaction to this period's elaborate designs. In America the style did not run parallel to the reign of Queen Anne (1702-1714), but first asserted itself around 1730 and remained popular for thirty years.

After the explosion of the ornament in the William and Mary style, the Queen Anne period was relatively staid, emphasizing simplicity in surface orna-

ment and gently curving, S-shaped lines, typified by the cabriole leg. Such organic forms stand in marked contrast to the architectural carvings of the previous period. Hardwoods such as walnut and mahogany were used. Ornament was applied sparingly, perhaps manifested in a simple carved shell ornament on the front of a chest. The style had a quiet elegance about it, combining a sense of simplicity and sophistication.

The Queen Anne period is generally regarded in decorative arts circles as the time when regional features became strongly noted in American furniture and

Shelburne Museum, Shelburne, Vermont

Delicacy was the hallmark of the Queen Anne era, and Vermont House at the Shelburne Museum captures this quality in its room collections. In a corner of the parlor, a gaming table and chairs lend a refined air; to the right, a cherry-wood lowboy with leaf-and-flower carving is an elegant complement to a japanned looking-glass.

the craftsman's skill reached new heights. At this time in New England, a technique known as blocking—by which a piece of wood was cut to create depressions and raised areas was developed. In Newport, Rhode Island—by then a popular residence of prosperous New Englanders—the Goddard and Townsend cabinetmaker families designed gorgeous blockfront case furniture. These pieces were ornamented with carved fan or shell motifs and elegant oval claw-and-ball-foot designs.

The refinements of the Queen Anne style were a response to the growing sophistication of Colonial life. As Marvin D. Schwartz observes in *American Furniture of the Colonial Period*, "By about 1730 tea-drinking had been transformed from a medicinal practice to a ritual of hospitality. For serving tea, small occasional tables were introduced." In addition to dainty, round and rectangular tea tables and card tables, the upholstered slipper chair and the sofa, which boasted graceful cabriole legs, were introduced during the Queen Anne period. Elaborate "cathedral paneling" on walls—carved decorations indicating window and column forms, as on a church wall—provided a suitable backdrop for such lovely pieces.

*The virtuoso skill of
the Yankee crafts-
man is reflected in this
chair from the Langdon
House collection (top).
A settee such as this
one (bottom) with ball-
and-claw feet would be a
stately complement to a
Chippendale interior.*

Without this cross-fertilization, it was possible for region-specific styles to emerge. Also, there was always a lapse between the time a style enjoyed popularity in Europe and when it arrived on the New World's shores. This can lead to confusion now in naming the stylistic periods of American furniture, as they do not correspond to European time periods.

In *American Furniture at Chipstone*, Oswaldo Rodriguez Roque addresses the problems of assigning furniture to all-encompassing categories: "To speak of 'a style' immediately brings to mind a given historical period, some general characteristics of appearance, and a defined sensibility strongly associated with the period in question. Yet this… overlooks or misunderstands those objects whose looks are not altogether comprehended by the definition, or which, although contemporaneous with the objects that do fit the norm, do not share their aesthetic." We should bear this in mind when referring to the "William and Mary," "Queen Anne," or "Chippendale" periods in American furniture—it is only for lack of a better or more appropriate terminology that these categories are used.

Around 1760, the tide turned slightly again with the advent of the Chippendale style, which was slightly more ornate than the Queen Anne. This style is named for Thomas Chippendale, the British cabinetmaker who published a book called *Gentlemen and Cabinet-Maker's Directory* in 1754. It culled the

42

most popular and up-to-the-minute furniture designs of England and the Continent, and American furniture makers used it only as a springboard for their own ideas.

Less cohesive than its predecessor and more whimsical, the Chippendale style incorporated Chinese motifs, typified by straight legs and frames on tables and chairs; Gothic elements, such as cluster-column legs and pointed arch forms in the backs of chairs; and French rococo swirls and scrolls called *rocaille*. These forms were uniquely interpreted in Massachusetts "kettle," or *bombé*, furniture, which had bulging bases.

In Newport, the Goddard and Townsend families continued with great success to produce furniture, which took on such fanciful touches as urn-shaped finials, scroll feet and claw-and-ball feet that emphasized the individual talons sharply (a popular holdover from the Queen Anne period), and blockfront furniture with a triple-shell motif—two carved convex shells on either side of one concave. New furniture forms of the Chippendale period included the Pembroke table, a breakfast table with fold-down leaves; and candlestands, diminutive circular tables (some with tilt tops to fold away for easy storage) designed to hold candlesticks. The addition of such specialized furniture forms to the American design repertoire indicated increasing refinement in the New England home.

Federal to Empire

Following the year 1788, the mood in America changed. The Constitution had been adopted, and there was a new feeling of independence. In England, Robert Adam had promoted the neo-classical style earlier in the century, but Americans had not gotten around to interpreting it in their own manner until this point. Neoclassicism repre-sented a return to classical elements in interior furnishings (as well as architecture) and the application of Greco-Roman motifs to furniture.

In the Old World, this period is associated with Hepplewhite and Sheraton designs, and these names are sometimes applied to American furniture. In the United States, this phase is known as the Federal Period and it ran (roughly) from 1780 to 1840. In New England, the architect-designer Samuel McIntire's contribution to furniture was significant. Working out of Salem, Massachusetts, which had risen as a shipping port and in turn gave rise to a wealthy citizenry, McIntire produced carved furniture with such decorative motifs as baskets of fruit and flowers, wheat sheaves, urns, and laurels. Connecticut craftsmen also rose in prominence, designing cherry-wood furniture ornamented with heraldic motifs. Rhode Island furniture makers developed a chair back with a Grecian "kylix" design—an urn with two graceful arching shapes emanating from it.

The later period of the Federal style, from 1820–1840, incorporates the Empire style, in which furniture in general became even more exuberant and romantic. Nationalistic icono-graphy in the form of eagles and shields became a very common motif. Stencil-ing was also used liberally on "fancy chairs," and was applied to Hitchcock chairs, which were produced in Hitchcockville, Connecticut, today called Riverton. Made of birch or maple with rush or plank seats, these chairs had elaborately turned stretchers and were used to furnish homes not only in New England but across America. Stenciling in general was a popular art form from the late-eighteenth into the early-nineteenth century, and poorer families used it instead of wallpaper to decorate their homes.

The Nineteenth Century

© Robert Perron

© Robert Perron

As communication and travel improved in nineteenth-century America, there was greater mixing of design ideas. Accordingly, New England furniture design became a less distinctive vernacular as the century progressed. Unusually enough, one distinct mode of furniture design practiced widely in New England did emerge in the nineteenth century—the Shaker style. Created by a group of religious dissidents, these furniture designs were characterized by their lack of ornament, clean lines, careful adherence to proportion, simplicity, and unselfconsciousness—a marked difference from the cluttered world of Victorian bric-a-brac. The most representative object is the classic and familiar Shaker chair, with its sturdy ladderback. Only useful elements were incorporated into Shaker designs.

Charles Dickens visited a Shaker village in 1842 and was unimpressed, writing in *American Notes* that everything seemed quite grim. He decried a culture that would, ''pluck from maturity and age their pleasant ornaments, and make existence but a narrow path towards the grave.'' Of course, today many people feel differently, and Shaker pieces—both authentic and reproduction—are appreciated for their beauty.

Despite the range of styles associated with New England, the styles share a common bond. All were created with characteristic Yankee pride and craftsmanship and bear a distinctively New England stamp in their basic sturdiness and imaginative designs.

© Brian Vanden Brink

Shaker pegs—many of which measured less than a half inch long—were used as window and drawer pulls as well as on pegboards and clock doors (page 44, top). Craftspeople still produce authentic designs with painstaking care. Here, a craftsman turns a peg in the traditional manner (page 44, bottom). At Sabbathday Lake—a Shaker community in Maine—even such simple household objects as brooms are elegantly designed. The spare, unpretentious elegance of Shaker design imbues every room (this page).

45

The New England interior has traditionally been filled with an eyecatching yet useful array of objects. Brass candlesticks were designed in endless variations (this page, left). Cooking implements were often displayed in the Colonial cupboard (this page, right). A Chinese export porcelain "Hong Bowl" depicts the flags of several nations that had set up trading headquarters in Canton in the eighteenth century (page 47, left). New Englanders also ornamented their homes with stenciled designs. Naturalistic and heraldic motifs were popular from Colonial to Federal times (page 47, right).

Brass candlesticks and candleholders

Standing about six to eight inches high, these utilitarian objects range from basic panstyle designs to more ornamental upright types with sculpted forms.

Broad staircases

Impressive staircases located in the entry hall were a popular feature of upper-class homes during the Georgian period in New England. Trios of carved balusters—often made of white pine—ornamented each step.

Clocks

In the eighteenth century, many New England homes acquired clocks —from massive grandfather types to mantel clocks. Often, they were carved to resemble the pediments over doorways or to depict a typical New England scene.

Cookware displays

Polished pewter and brass cooking implements and burl bowls were traditionally kept by the hearth for ready access, but now they make great decorative elements in the kitchen and dining room.

Fieldstone and brick fireplaces

The New England hearth was initially a necessity for cooking and warmth and later developed into an ornamental feature—although it was still just as practical. In the earliest homes, the fieldstone hearth was common, while later the brick fireplace—or chimney oven—was added to the kitchen. Fireplaces were generally massive, and as interiors became more sophisticated, they were often adorned with decorative mantelpieces surrounded by elaborate carving.

Marbleized, feathered, and grained walls

In the eighteenth century, wealthy homeowners commissioned these fanciful painting techniques to simulate the look of other materials. Any number of colors were used—for instance feathered walls might be done in a gray-and-muted-red combination. These techniques are still used to make coveted New England interiors.

Oil lamps

Whales were once so plentiful off the New England coast that their oil was used as cheap fuel for lamps. There are many different designs of oil lamps to choose from, such as wineglass courting lamps, which were burned when women entertained courters, and ship's lamps. Use them to decorate walls and windowsills.

Oriental porcelain displays

Inexpensive Oriental porcelain became a staple of New England homes in the eighteenth century. Part of the reason for the influx was the tea trade with the East, and exports from Canton, China, flooded the New World. Much of this porcelain was painted with heraldic American motifs. The porcelain is typically displayed in a cupboard.

Paneling and fancy woodwork

In wealthier homes of the Georgian period and thereafter, particularly in Connecticut, intricately carved and deeply recessed wood paneling was an important decorative motif and was often displayed in the parlor. Sometimes referred to as cathedral paneling because it tended to be divided in sections resembling church windows, it also echoed the lines of the hearth. This paneling would also extend to doors—in the form of lintels and moldings—and to cupboards, often with scalloped shelves and in an arch, dome, or shell shape.

Stenciling

Many early-nineteenth-century middle-class homes featured walls stenciled by itinerant artists in a variety of designs. Stenciling took little time to do and was less expensive than wallpapers. Kits are widely available today for do-it-yourself stencilers.

Creating a Historic New England Interior

Richard Eustace practices interior design in New England by striking a delicate balance between the past and the present. Drawing on a scholastic background in art history and the decorative arts as well as a working background in creating period rooms for museums, Eustace designs with a comprehensive view of the styles and artistic movements of the past and the many possibilities for pulling rooms together drawing on the visual expressions of different eras. With these various elements in place, he decided to combine his talents and visual penchant for the past to interior decoration.

Practicing from Boston in his firm, Atlantic House, Eustace undertakes the furnishing of homes of all sorts in New England. There are many approaches to design, but first and foremost for Eustace is the house itself:

"I think you have to let the house speak to you. Successful interiors respect—or don't disrespect—the historical integrity of the space they're being put into."

This means that the designer must consider the scale of the rooms and select furniture—whether modern or period—that works comfortably within it.

For owners of period New England homes, it can often be challenging to design the interior because one feels compelled to design within the period. Rather than seeing this as a burden, why not approach it with a detective-like curiosity. Eustace has a number of tips for finding clues to the early character of the house and its owners. Some good methods are to track down genealogy to get a sense of the personalities of generations of owners, and looking at the broader social picture of the time (such as the fashions), paint analysis, and photographs.

Eustace feels that this detective path is worth pursuing since you never know what it will turn up. And so when he approaches a period home, not only does he follow his first rule—letting the house speak to him—but he also undertakes a study of the house: "Sometimes it's interesting to do a scientific paint analysis. I like to look at layers of wallpaper in out-of-the-way places—in backs of cupboards, under the stairs, places where they might have forgotten to repaper. It's interesting to look at and use that information to get an idea of the original design intent."

Tracking down photographs of the house from the past can also be remarkably useful. Says Eustace, "One of the other things I've been amused to do when I'm working on houses that I know had been photographed is to go to the Society for the Preservation of New England Antiquities and search their photo archives. On two separate occasions I've found photos that have allowed me to see how people chose to arrange furniture. Sometimes you're confronted with houses with odd halls, rooms with too many doorways, or too many pathways through the living room. You may sit and play with plans on paper and suddenly find in a photo the solution: perhaps an interesting piece of furniture that could redirect a room flow."

One of the advantages of working in New England is being able to draw on the skills of craftsmen there—continuing the traditions begun so long ago. And so, when architectural details need to be added to a home, Eustace is able to realize his design vision. "We use good builders and custom cabinet shops. I think that we're very lucky to have a lot of skilled tradesmen here. They know how to replicate architectural details and how to restore woodwork or millwork." Eustace had practiced interior design elsewhere in the country and had disappointing

Interior designer Richard Eustace oriented this room around the hearth, in the traditional New England manner (page 49). The furnishings are evocative of the past, yet are contemporary and durable enough to give the room a comfortable air.

experiences with tradespeople who found such approaches too time-intensive to be worth the trouble.

To bring a period flavor to rooms, it is often necessary to add reproduction elements. In doing so, Eustace strives to achieve a blended look: "When adding architectural elements—new book-cases, a paneled door in the Georgian mode, or a fireplace surround—we look at the house itself and search for clues for how to reconstruct or add on such features. I hope they will look as if they had been there."

Of course, there are a limited number of period homes available graced with such architectural flourishes, and many people must opt to buy contemporary homes. For Eustace, this does not preclude the presence of antiques. For new houses or houses that have pre-existing contemporary furniture that must be integrated with a few older pieces, Eustace finds several solutions: "I like the Federal period—including Sheraton and Hepplewhite—with its elegance and spare line. I think those furnishings work very well with con-

*F*ramed vintage
drawings and
several eye-catching
objets *impart a serene,*
timeless quality to this
contemporary New
England study.

temporary upholstered furnishings.
And they have an architectural quality
that translates to a variety of rooms."

When it comes to actually furnishing
a room with antiques, Eustace feels that
the "decorative arts approach"—in
which all materials are carefully assem-
bled and all pertain to that period—of
museums is too confining. Although
Eustace acknowledges that this style has
been popular in the past, he feels that
period rooms can end up looking dry:
"People today are willing to be a little
more eclectic and prefer rooms that
are more 'real,'" which means that
furniture of different periods can be
used to decorate the same room in a
realistic approach that reflects the way
people really live.

Eustace is of the opinion that quality
pieces of good design can be freely
mixed, so long as the effect is not jar-
ring: "Carefully done, with an eye to
scale and proportion and similarity of
line and texture and surface, I think you
can do surprising things in mixing
furniture from different periods."

In designing for clients, Eustace likes
to take an incremental approach. If
they already own furniture that they
want to incorporate into a new design
scheme, this is perfectly permissible.
"Even if people have second-string
kinds of things, we build a framework
to showcase those possessions to best
advantage. I like old patinas and am not
worried about the tabletop that's a little
dented. It's nice to work with family
pieces because the result doesn't look
so 'decorated' and store-bought."

A client might acquire an outstand-
ing piece of furniture that inspires him
or her to completely redecorate. As
often is the case, Eustace will build a
room around such "significant" pieces
—a great secretary desk, for example.

"In the household of the Notch he found warmth and simplicity of feeling, the pervading intelligence of New England, and a poetry of native growth…"
—*Nathaniel Hawthorne*, from "The Ambitious Guest", The Celestial Railroad and Other Stories

It is not only furniture that brings a period room to life but the accessories as well. Period pottery, glassware, or sculpture can become the benchmark of the room and can completely set the tone. For example, a collection of Bennington pottery on a mantelpiece might be something to base an entire design of a room on. This is especially significant if you have a limited budget but want to convincingly achieve the look of a period interior. Says Eustace, "I strongly recommend period accessories—porcelain, lampbases that can be rewired, prints—for a room rather than buying mass-market things or things for decoration market. Period accessories give a room a different air."

Another way to achieve an antique look without buying a lot of expensive furniture is to add small details to a room that evoke the past. Eustace says that such a detail might be a mirror hung between windows or over a fireplace. Such details, he says, can evoke "a quiet sense of the past" without a slavish copying of an entire period's style.

As for the other furnishings of the room, upholstery and draperies, Eustace feels that textiles that evoke the feeling of the period can greatly enhance a room: "There are times when it's interesting to be purist. For instance, I'm working on a house with eighteenth- to nineteenth-century folk art and wonderful nautical antiques. To complement the decor, we're using ultrafine worsted wools, coarsely loomed fabrics, and rough-textured linens—all upholstery fabrics used in the last century."

For those people who wish to collect New England furniture and accessories but don't know how to begin, Eustace feels that the only way to acquire an eye is to examine the furniture firsthand: "To train your aesthetic, nothing is more useful than simply comparing and contrasting. Develop your eye: look and look. A lot of people won't go to a particular show or shop because they feel it is too expensive. But you should go to the dealers that have the finest things and look and take that information away with you so that when you're at the country shop or local auction house, you might recognize the proverbial diamond in the rough or something that's been miscatalogued."

Among the furniture styles that Eustace feels are the least pricey for their quality are the seventeenth-century styles, William and Mary furniture, and generally, furniture made before 1750. The Federal style has skyrocketed in price, as has much nineteenth-century furniture.

To separate the wheat from the chaff, Eustace again recommends careful examination of objects: "Get an eye for a hand-rubbed finish as opposed to a factory-made one. Understand what hand carving and hand painting looks like, or how to tell the difference between real gold leaf and metal leaf." This is not something that can be conveyed in words, Eustace cautions. It can only be learned through building a "visual memory" through firsthand experience.

© Eric Roth

Quirky yet not necessarily expensive pieces of furniture can transform a living space. In this room, a child's chair and a trunk add a visual element of surprise. The nautical theme established by the ship figurehead is reinforced by the framed art over the mantelpiece, and the flag-waving "Crackerjack" sailor on the side table.

© Eric Roth

NEW ENGLAND FOODS

New England's earliest white settlers probably owe their lives to the Native Americans who helped them through their first hard years on the new continent. The first winter the Pilgrims ate from the land and from their new neighbors' stores. As soon as they could, however, the Pilgrims planted twenty acres of maize and a few acres each of English wheat and peas. The European seeds failed to sprout, forcing the refugees farther away from their English traditions and more toward the simple bounty of the land.

Most of us grew up accepting the myth that the Pilgrims readily changed their habits and

*tastebuds, adopting the new ways with relish.
Yankee cooking, the simple, delicious cuisine
that developed out of Native American cooking,
didn't become popular until the late 1700s or
the early 1800s. Until then, the Pilgrims
tenaciously held on to the cooking styles of
the old country.*

*Revisionist history notwithstanding,
New England is home to a long list of fine
delicacies. From the ocean come cod, scrod,
lobster, oysters, clams, mussels, and shad.
From the land, beans and corn, cranberries
and apples, fiddlehead ferns and the sweet sap
of the sugar maple. And New England foods
still figure prominently in many kitchens.
With a nod to the past, chefs are whipping up
just barely altered versions of boiled dinners,
clambakes, and Thanksgiving feasts with
Indian pudding, cranberry sauce, and maple
desserts. The pages that follow can only begin
to bring you the building blocks of a long-
standing tradition.*

© Hanson Carroll/FPG International

56

*N*ew England food to some people is synonymous with traditional fare (page 54), but the region's cuisine goes far beyond simple roast fowl. Clambakes, with loads of steamed fresh lobster and clams, are always popular along the New England coast (this page, top). As important as fowl and sea fare, corn (below) and corn meal—once called Indian meal—figured in johnnycakes, steamed bread, puddings, fritters, and more.

57

© Envision

© Ronald Partis/Envision

Buckets collect maple syrup as it runs in the spring (this page). Maple syrup (opposite) comes in many grades. The lightest—Grade A Amber in most states—is the most delicate and best for pancakes. Grade C, a dark cooking syrup stands in contrast; thick and heady, it is rarely for sale in supermarkets. Look for it instead at sugar orchards; it's usually sold in big jugs at half the price of Grade A.

MAPLE SYRUP

When the snow melts with a ferocity that bites into the land and floods tree trunks to ankle depth or more, it's mud season; and sometime just before mud season hits full force, when the sap begins to run in the sugar maples, about mid-February to the end of March, it's sugaring time. As quickly as the sun goes down, the temperature plunges back into the realm of chilly winter. These warm days and freezing nights mark the time when only a few sugarers escape with a full night's sleep. In an average season, sap drips into the buckets drop by drop, maybe totalling a half-gallon on a good day, but there have been nights when the sap poured out of the tree spigots like a cascade, making the 16-quart-metal buckets look like saucepans catching ceiling drips in a hurricane.

Years when sap production races ahead of the boiling process come only so often, but sugarers are a tenacious lot. They stay with sugaring despite the fact that most still have to set up and retrieve their buckets on snowshoe or in heavy boots, hoisting and heaving filled containers that could—but don't often—spill. They keep the fires going, sometimes all night long, to boil the sap until it becomes the rich auburn syrup that no self-respecting Yankee would turn down.

Legend has it that maple syrup was discovered by a young Native American warrior who after a hard day left his tomahawk embedded in the bark of a sugar maple. As the weather warmed the next morning, the sap ran down the tomahawk into a wooden trough that happened to be beneath the tree. Enjoying the warmth of the day, the warrior's wife neglected to fetch water for her pot and instead used the tree water. As the tree water boiled it sweetened the meat in the pot, and maple syrup hooked its first devotee.

FOODS

"I saw that I could easily raise my bushel or two of rye and Indian corn... and if I must have some concentrated sweet, I found by experiment that I could make a very good molasses either of pumpkins or beets, and I knew that I needed only to set out a few maples to obtain it more easily still."
—H. D. Thoreau, Walden

"I am led to expect," wrote a prominent figure in 1791, "that a material part of the general happiness which heaven seems to have prepared for mankind, will be derived from the manufacture and general use of Maple Sugar." The delicate complexity of real maple syrup can't be duplicated, and in no place else does the sap run as sweet and as willingly as in the northeastern states and provinces of North America.

Harry Morse runs a farm and sugar operation "about three miles just up above Montpelier on a hill." He remembers: "I started boiling sap when I could hardly look over the edge of the evaporating pan," a good seventy years ago. To hear his story, not too much has changed since the days when wooden buckets attached to shoulder yokes and iron kettles held the syrup. The Morse family still burns wood for the fires that transform approximately forty gallons of sap into one gallon of syrup. Though factory-made evaporator pans have taken the place of the kettles, and covered metal buckets have replaced wooden ones, most of the daily routine requires footwork and constant visits to the trees.

Sugaring knowledge passed down from generation to generation isn't likely to get lost; it gets refined, as in the case of David Marvin, who like Harry Morse, learned sugaring from his father. Marvin, however, has catapulted the trade into a new age. Plastic tubing directly affixed to the trees catches the sap and directs it to the sugarhouse. The machines at his Butternut Mountain Farm in Johnson, Vermont, were originally developed to desalinate seawater. A clever skip of the imagination led Marvin to use the reverse-osmosis machine, as it's called, to separate out the water molecules from the all-important sugar and flavor molecules. He ends up with a very sweet concentrate that he boils down to syrup, a technique that saves energy efficiently without loss of flavor. "Instead of using four and a half gallons of fuel oil [in place of wood], we now use about three quarts. At the same time, our evaporator, which normally produces about seven or eight gallons of syrup an hour now yields about thirty."

Both men, each of a different generation, fondly recall the greatest of all maple traditions: sugar on snow. You simply boil the syrup until it spins a thread, to about 232°F. Don't stir it, just pour it out onto fresh snow or shaved ice. It'll thicken like taffy—and get stuck in your teeth more than taffy—and taste divine. Serve it with a sour pickle and a sweet doughnut!

Marvin's Maple Oatmeal Cookies

1 1/4 cups margarine or butter

1/2 cup granulated maple sugar

1/2 cup granulated white sugar

1 egg

1 teaspoon vanilla

1/2 cup flour

1 teaspoon baking soda

1 teaspoon salt

1 teaspoon cinnamon

1/4 teaspoon nutmeg

3 cups rolled oats (not instant)

Preheat the oven to 375°F.

In a large bowl, cream together the margarine or butter and sugars. Beat in the egg and vanilla and mix well. In a separate bowl, mix together the flour, baking soda, salt, cinnamon, and nutmeg. Stir the combined dry ingredients into the butter mixture and mix well. Then stir in the oats. Drop on an ungreased cookie sheet and bake for 8 to 9 minutes.

Yields 18 cookies

Creamy Maple Cashew Bark

1 1/2 cups maple syrup

1 1/2 cups unsalted cashew nuts, lightly toasted

2 to 3 tablespoons butter

1 teaspoon baking soda

Lightly butter a baking sheet and set it aside. Combine the maple syrup and nuts in a large, heavy pan and slowly bring to a simmer over medium heat. Cook, stirring as little as possible, until the mixture reads 270°F on a candy thermometer. Stir in the butter and remove the pan from the heat.

Quickly stir in the baking soda, which will make the mixture foam. Pour it at once onto the prepared sheet and use the back of the spoon to spread the candy as thinly as possible. Allow it to cool, then break the bark into pieces. Store in an airtight tin.

Yields two dozen pieces

61

JOHNNYCAKES, CLAMCAKES, AND INDIAN PUDDING

Early recipes for Indian pudding (opposite) called for cooking the corn mixture in stonelined underground ovens, or brick ovens, to insure a slow, steady heat. When sailors returned from their voyages in the 1800s, many brought back tapioca, which required much less time to cook than corn.

The Native Americans of the northeastern woodlands began cultivating maize, or corn, about 1,500 years ago, a change in habit that led these hunters to farming. By a still unexplained quirk in the plant's development, Indian corn (*Zea mays*) needs a farmer's help to propagate. The plant cannot spread its seeds until a person husks the ears, exposes the kernels, and sows them as seeds.

Without corn, the Pilgrims would have starved that first winter in Massachusetts. The story goes that each person received only five precious kernels each day during the period of famine. Governor William Bradford wrote: "In April of the first year they began to plant their corne, in which service Squanto stood them in great stead, showing them both ye manner how to set it, and after, how to dress and tend it." Squanto was a Pawtuxet tribe member who had been spirited away to England, then returned, years before. In Europe, he acquired an education that allowed him to translate between the Pilgrims and the Native Americans. Tisquantum, as he was also called, taught the white settlers how to pound the corn and transform it into a kind of cornmeal pancake we now call johnnycake.

When Benjamin Franklin wrote that "…johny or hoecake, hot from the fire, is better than a Yorkshire muffin," little did he know that he was skirting the edge of a great debate. For in Rhode Island *jonnycakes* are never spelled with an *h* nor eaten with maple syrup; while in the rest of New England, the *h* is as evident as the sweet topping. Rhode Islanders take their tradition to heart. Not only do they have a Society for the Propagation of the Jonnycake Tradition in Rhode Island (SPJTRI)—and a good sense of humor!—but they also have a

handful of old mills that are still producing stone-ground corn. Purists contend that johnnycakes must be made with native Rhode Island white cap or flint corn, which, says miller Tim McTague, is "harder to grow, has a longer season, and is harder to harvest but has a nutty and sweet oily taste that generally sets it apart from other corns."

No one knows for sure how these cornmeal pancakes got their name. Most folks say the word is a corruption of "journey cake," named because colonial travelers could cook up a batch, pack them in their saddlebags, and heat them up over a campfire or eat them plain when they were ready to sup on the road. Another story claims the word comes from the Shawnee Indians: "Shawnee cake." However the dish came by its name, it follows the Native American tradition of adding water to the cornmeal, patting the mixture into flat cakes, and baking them in or near the fire.

Taking note of Native American techniques, the settlers began to build mills in the late 1600s, using water or wind to power the operation. The tradition continues in slightly altered form to this day at both Gray's and Kenyon's, whose mill sites are thought to date back to the seventeenth century. While Gray's still grinds the flint corn, Kenyon's is perhaps better known for its fritter and batter mix, which cooks up some of the best clamcakes around.

Every September in West Springfield, Massachusetts, business people, farmers, dairymen, children, and the curious by the thousands gather at the Eastern States Exposition. Bordering the grounds on one side is a row of truly "stately" buildings that represent the states of Maine, New Hampshire, Vermont, Connecticut, Massachusetts,

"She told me of her household occupations, that she made all their bread, because her father liked only hers; then saying shyly, 'And people must have their puddings,' this very timidly and suggestively, as if they were meteors or comets."
— *Thomas Wentworth Higginson* on Emily Dickinson, from Selected Poems and Letters of Emily Dickinson. Edited by Robert N. Linscott

and Rhode Island. It's possible to eat your way through New England without ever leaving the street. Massachusetts' apples, Connecticut's milk, Vermont's cotton-candy-like spun maple, and for the main course, Rhode Island clamcakes or clam fritters from Kenyon's. In a good year, says Kenyon's owner Paul Drumm, they "cook up 6½ tons of the clamcake mix for 1 million visitors."

Recipes for Indian pudding show up all over the Northeast. Amelia Simmons, author of what is considered the first American cookbook, aptly named *American Cookery* and published in Connecticut, included three versions of "A Nice Indian Pudding." And Alice Morse Earle wrote in *Home Life in Colonial Days* that "the hard Indian pudding slightly sweetened and boiled in a bag was everywhere made. It was told that many New England families had three hundred and sixty-five such puddings in a year." Puritan families wanting to preserve the sabbath on Sunday made Indian pudding the day before. Many times it held a prominent place on the supper table, but just as often it served as the first course of the day.

The delectable dessert melts on the tongue. With a dollop of vanilla ice cream, you have a treat that is hot and cold, grainy and smooth. The sweetness is less an assault on the mouth than a seduction. A heady aroma surrounds the cooking process, weaving almost visible cinnamon-scented clouds into the air. Traditionally the cornmeal pudding was baked or boiled, made with eggs or without, dotted with raisins or not, and sweetened with molasses or maple syrup. Some recipes call for tapioca, baking soda, or white flour; some require three hours of baking, others five to seven hours, and still others only one hour. There are probably as many recipes as there are traditional New England cooks.

Thick Johnnycakes

2 cups johnnycake meal

2 cups boiling water

1 teaspoon salt

$^1/_4$ cup milk

1 teaspoon sugar (optional)

Mix together the meal, boiling water, and salt. Let stand 5 minutes. Stir in the milk. Oil a skillet well and heat to medium-hot. Fry 2$^1/_2$-inch cakes until browned, then flip and brown again.

Note: For thin Johnnycakes substitute $^3/_4$ cup *cold* water for the boiling water, and increase the milk to 1$^1/_2$ cups.

Yields 12 johnnycakes

Indian Pudding

6 cups milk

1 cup yellow cornmeal

2 eggs

$^1/_2$ cup dark unsulphered molasses

4 tablespoons unsalted butter, at room temperature

$^1/_4$ cup sugar

$1^1/_2$ teaspoons cinnamon

$1^1/_2$ teaspoons nutmeg

$^1/_2$ teaspoon salt

$^1/_4$ teaspoon baking powder

Preheat the oven to 300°F. Grease a $1^1/_2$- to 2-quart casserole or soufflé dish, preferably with butter. Mix together the cornmeal, eggs, molasses, butter, sugar, cinnamon, salt, and baking powder. Stir until well blended; set aside. Scald the milk in a thick saucepan. Using a wire whisk, blend the milk gradually into the cornmeal mixture. Transfer the pudding back to the saucepan and cook, stirring continuously, for approximately 2 minutes until it just reaches a low boil. Remove from the stove and pour into the casserole.

Fill a roasting pan or high-edged cake pan with enough water to cover the bottom of the casserole. Set the casserole pan in the water-filled pan on the middle shelf of the oven. Bake for $3^1/_2$ to 4 hours, replenishing the water as necessary.

Serve the pudding warm with a scoop of vanilla ice cream or a generous drizzle of heavy cream.

Serves 6 to 8

Clamcakes
a.k.a. Clam Fritters

1 box Kenyon's Fritter Mix

1 cup canned minced clams or quahogs with juice

Combine the fritter mix, clams and juice, and 1 to $1^1/_2$ cups of water and mix well. Continue to add water until the batter is spoonable but not soupy. (The amount of water to use varies with the amount of clam juice added.) Drop the batter by the teaspoonful—the size of a golf ball—into a fryer at 350°F. The fritters will sink to the bottom for a few seconds before bobbing to the top of the fryer. Turn the fritters gently while cooking for 3 to 4 minutes or until light brown. Remove with a slotted spoon and drain on a paper towel placed over a brown bag.

Serves 2

A Nice Indian Pudding.

No. 1. 3 pints scalded milk, 7 spoons fine Indian meal, stir well together while hot, let stand till cooled; add 7 eggs, half pound raisins, 4 ounces butter, spice and sugar, bake one and half hour.

No. 2. 3 pints scalded milk to one pint meal salted; cool, add 2 eggs, 4 ounces butter, sugar or molasses and spice q.s. it will require two and half hours baking.

No. 3. Salt a pint meal, wet with one quart milk, sweeten and put into a strong cloth, brass or bell metal vessel, stone or earthen pot, secure from wet and boil 12 hours.

—the original text from the 1796 edition of Amelia Simmons's American Cookery, or the Art of Dressing Viands, Fish, Poultry and Vegetables, and the Best Modes of Making Pastes, Puffs, Pies, Tarts, Puddings, Custards and Preserves, and all Kinds of Cakes, from the Imperial Plumb to Plain Cake Adapted to this Country, and all Grades of Life

Most clam fritters (page 66)—or clamcakes—are made with "quahogs," as Yankees call big clams. Quahogs provided the original wampum shells, Merceneria mercenaris (also known as hard-shell or littleneck clams in some circles). Recipes for fiddlehead ferns (this page) don't often appear in cookbooks; the recipes get handed down by word of mouth. Enterprising young chefs, however, are discovering new ways to prepare them, using them as greens in salads and appetizers, and even in gumbo and tempura. Clambakes (opposite) rival boiled dinners as the preeminent New England entree.

© Steven Mark Needham/ Envision

FIDDLEHEAD FERNS

Yankee reticence. It's an old stereotype that doesn't always hold up. Sometimes it does; just ask anyone where they pick their fiddlehead ferns, and you're likely to get a reluctant answer: "Oh, along riverbanks and floodplains."

"Can you be more specific?" you might ask.

"Nope."

If someone's in a good mood he or she may allow that the tender young sprouts of ferns poke up in areas where little else grows at the time, so the fiddleheads—named because they resemble the curled neck of a violin— are noticeable. One New Hampshire native admitted only that she "just happened to come across them" when she was out looking for rare plants.

Found in New England, primarily in Maine, New Hampshire and Vermont, fiddleheads aren't endangered or rare. They're just edible for such a short time that no one wants to share them. Collectors are limited to about two weeks in early May to gather the greens. After that the tightly furled fronds open into mature ostrich ferns (*Matteuccia struthiotteris*). The sudden spurt of growth that transforms the fiddleheads into recognizable ferns is legendary. One old Mainer said he saw a fiddlehead grow two inches in one day.

All ferns are called fiddleheads when they come up curled, but only the ostrich fern—and some say the cinnamon fern (*Osmunda cinnamonea*)—is good and safe to eat.

Before cooking the fiddleheads, which resemble modern-day birthday whizzers which uncurl and extend with a good breath, as much as violin necks, you must defuzz them. The most reliable method seems to be washing the ferns, then wiping them with a damp paper towel. Steam or boil the greens for 3 to 10 minutes, then run cold water over them quickly to stop the cooking process. (The shorter cooking time reflects the modern trend to serve vegetables al dente.) Squeeze a lemon over them, and they're done.

If you like canned asparagus, you might like canned fiddleheads; otherwise, don't mistake the packaged ferns for the real thing.

CLAMBAKES

You must have no shame when eating a freshly steamed lobster. Attack it with gusto. Forget any pretensions, dress down, and summon the joys of childhood summers (even if you lived a thousand miles from the nearest whiff of salt water!). My mother often tells the story of two men transfixed, watching me unswervingly devour a lobster at the tender age of three. I had mastered the art, beginning with the small legs and working through the claws to the tail. Nothing could deter me. That hasn't changed. Neither has the clambake.

The clambake is a tradition in the truest sense of the word, handed down from one generation to the next and even from one culture to the next. As with many New England traditions, the clambake traces its roots to the Native Americans, who had refined the art of cooking seafood and corn over hot stones long before the Pilgrims showed

up. The first organized settlers' clambake, however, apparently took place near Dartmouth, Massachusetts, as part of a Quaker Sunday-school picnic. The white newcomers presumably did little to improve upon the Native Americans' well-established method, and our current seaside bakes differ only perhaps in the Frisbee™ game that now serves to work up a good appetite.

A clambake, in short, is a steamed one-pot or one-pit dinner of clams, sweet corn, onions, new potatoes, lobsters (if affordable), and sausage (optional). Its essence, however, whether on the beach or at home, lies in the subtle blending of flavors produced by the steam as it rises from the bottom layer of seaweed up.

The best clambakes are outside. Nothing can match the anticipation of watching the all-day preparations for the bake. Besides inviting people, there is no "first" rule, because it really

"To many creatures there is in this sense but one necessary of life, Food."
—H. D. Thoreau, Walden

69

Raw clams like these have made the waters off New England famous. They are the essential ingredient in every clambake, and you haven't really tasted a clam until you've tasted a fresh one.

© Burke/Triolo

depends on whether you plan to collect your main ingredients from the sea or purchase them at the local fish store. Digging a pit, however, tops most lists. Let's assume you expect twenty guests. The State of Maine Department of Sea and Shore Fisheries suggests digging a shallow, circular hole in the ground three feet in diameter and about eight to ten inches deep (although I've never seen anyone with a tape measure at

a clambake, and I have seen deeper holes!). Dig above the tideline, so you won't lose your meal to the waves. In the meantime, soak a large tarp in seawater.

While part of your crew is digging, send a company of others to collect hard, granitic, grapefruit- to football-sized rocks. Smooth, round or oval ones make it easier to keep a tidy bake. Stay away from sedimentary rocks such as flat sandstone; they can crumble or pop in the intense heat.

Children squeal at the thought of collecting the approximately twenty pounds of seaweed needed but rarely turn down the opportunity to get good and slimy. Make sure it's rockweed, a peculiar type of seaweed characterized by small water-filled bladders that are fun to pop and that provide much of the steam for the bake.

Adventures always ensue when you search for clams. You can be thigh-deep in water and wearing sneakers, or barefoot and walking the tidal flats; either way, the ocean often presents itself as a tangible guest. Be prepared to get wet. Collect or buy about a dozen clams per person. Scrub the outside of the clams, then put them in a large bucket of seawater (or one gallon of fresh water mixed with one cup of salt) with a few handfuls of cornmeal. Keep them cool and out of direct sunlight while you let them soak for several hours. Refresh the water and cornmeal a few times, rinsing the bucket thoroughly each time to remove sand and grit. Throw away any open clams.

Each person should also get a 1-to-1½-pound lobster, a new potato or two in the red jacket, a small peeled onion, and at least one ear of fresh sweet corn prepared so that all but the inner husk has been removed. Buy four to five pounds of Portuguese sausage (*chourica* or *linguica*) or Spanish chorizo, if desired. To make serving easier, put together a cheesecloth packet with potato, onion, and corn for every guest.

Now back to the pit. Line the hole with the rocks, making a somewhat level surface. To really follow the old customs, cut a six-foot length from a birch sapling and collect smaller, green twigs to make a broom that won't catch fire. Attach the smaller twigs to the sapling with a wire, as shown in the illustration. (Substituting a dry broom soaked in water will only take heat

away from the rocks; instead, use a green evergreen bough if you're not near birch trees.) Next sweep the rocks, clearing away as much sand and dirt as possible. You'll need about a quarter of a cord of wood cut into approximately sixteen-inch lengths.

Start the fire with a little kindling, then let it burn wide to encompass as many of the rocks as possible. The stones should be ready in two to three hours; to test, expose one or two with a shovel, pushing the wood to the side, and sprinkle on a few drops of water. It should sizzle and steam immediately (so be sure to stand out of the way as you do this to avoid getting burned). Working quickly, remove the hot wood and any coals with the shovel or a steel rake. (A metal trash can makes a good receptacle for the spent wood.) Sweep the rocks again, brushing away the remaining ashes and sand.

The drama unfolds. As you thoroughly line the pit with the rockweed —about six inches deep—precious steam will come billowing up out of the hole. Again, work quickly. Place the washed clams directly on the seaweed or on a half-inch wire-mesh screen that crosses the pit. Put the lobsters directly on top of the clams, then add the sausage (if you have it), onions, potatoes, and corn or the cheesecloth packets. Cover everything with the soaked tarp, then set heavy stones around the edges to keep it in place. (No part of the tarp should be touching the hot rocks.) Let it steam for about an hour.

To test for doneness, lift a small corner of the tarp with a heat-resistant mitt, being careful to avoid the steam. Check the closest lobster. If it's red, the clambake's ready, and you can serve directly from the pit.

One quick note on safety: wear shoes, socks, long pants, a long-sleeved shirt, and a heavy mitt or canvas gloves if you're a member of the pit crew. Fire and steam, like the ocean, should be respected.

"I have made a satisfactory dinner… simply of a dish of purslane (Portulaca oleracea) *which I gathered in my own cornfield, boiled and salted…And pray what more can a reasonable man desire, in peaceful times, in ordinary noons, than a sufficient number of ears of green sweet corn boiled, with the addition of salt?… Bread I at first made of pure Indian meal and salt, genuine hoe-cakes…"*
—H. D. Thoreau, Walden

FOODS

Individuals may quibble about whether the lobsters should crown the heap or how many layers of seaweed are necessary. They may boast of bakes in a barrel, a steel drum, or a stovepipe, all of which will do. The fundamentals, however, really do stay the same, and in fact, are easily translated to stovetop cookery (see recipe, page 73).

Table customs also rarely waver. Every two or three people should have access to paired bowls of fresh clam liquor and melted butter; empty bowls for discarding the shells; lobster crackers or small, clean, heavy rocks; lots of lemon; and piles of absorbent cloth napkins—or even terry-cloth dish towels.

To properly eat a steamed clam, extract it from the shell, which the heat will have opened. You'll see the clam in all its finery: an exposed and swollen belly attached to a thin, more muscular neck. A black sheath covers the neck; roll this off away from the belly and discard, then dip the entire clam first into the liquor to season it and wash away any remaining sand, then into the melted butter, which you can flavor with a few squeezes of lemon. With that done, just pop it into your mouth. Mmmm.

The lobster requires more time. Begin with the two rows of small legs; twist these off one at a time and simply suck the meat from them. Break the entire claw from the body, then, following the natural joints of the animal, break the claw itself from what old-timers call the knuckle and little kids call the arm. Mainers worth their salt will push the meat through the shell rather than cracking the armor. If you do crack it,

don't close the cracker completely; let it start the work that you can finish with your fingers. That way no shell flakes adhere to the supple meat.

Separate the tiny thumb claw from the big claw over a bowl. Water may come rushing out. A neat break will leave the smaller claw meat exposed. Again, push or crack to get at the large claw. (Perhaps the greatest debate in lobsterdom is over which meat is more delicious: the claw or the tail.)

For a less messy lobster, make a cut across the tail where it joins the body, then make another cut perpendicular to the first one along the length of the tail; alternatively, you can break the tail off and just push the meat through. Either way, be sure to extract the thin tasty slivers from the small fans at the very end of the lobster tail. I usually can't resist eating some of the tail at this time. Depending on the size of the lobster and the size of my appetite, I will next either attack the body or dispense with the labor-intensive work of sorting and sifting through the structure to get at the small pockets of meat, the roe, and for those of strong stomach, the liver (or tomalley). Whichever, I still save the tail —or most of it—for last.

Unfortunately, although lobsters were so plentiful in early Colonial days that it was considered embarrassing to offer *only* lobster, they are now disappearing from many small-town bakes because of their high cost.

Clambakes are more than just fun these days. Massachusetts, Rhode Island, and Maine communities have become famous for their fund-raising bakes; the tradition now also continues at a few commercial clambakes where guests sit at long tables and mingle with strangers and where it's not unusual for someone to end the meal with a sing-along—but not until the watermelon's served!

Stovetop Clambake

A large (about 18-quart) enamel pot with an interior perforated steamer is not essential, but it helps.

2 dozen cherrystone clams or steamers (soft-shell clams)

Handful of cornmeal

Approximately 15 pounds of wet rockweed (available, with advance notice, from fish stores)

8 small new (red) potatoes

4 small white onions

4 ears fresh sweet corn, unshucked

1 pound of Portuguese sausage (chourica or linguica) or Spanish chorizo

³/₄ cup white wine

1¹/₂ cups water

As with the outdoor clambake, scrub the outside of the clams, then put them in a large bowl of seawater (or 1 quart of fresh cold water mixed with 1 teaspoon of salt) with a handful or two of cornmeal. Soak in a cool area, away from direct sunlight for a few hours, refreshing the water and cornmeal intermittently. Each time you renew the salty water, rinse the bowl thoroughly to remove any sand or grit. Throw away any open clams.

Rinse the rockweed thoroughly, also, to remove any excess sand and grit. Line the bottom of the pot with a medium-thick layer of seaweed. Wash the potatoes and put all but two of them in a cheesecloth packet on top of the seaweed. Make cheesecloth packets of six clams for each person and place them on top of the potatoes. Skin the onions and put them in another cheesecloth packet on top of the clams. Shuck the outer layers of the corn and put them in the pot next. Finally add the lobsters (be sure to remove all the rubber bands, although the pegs can stay in). Cover with another, thinner layer of seawood. Top with the sausage and the two potatoes. Pour in the wine and water.

Cover tightly and bring the ingredients to a boil. Turn the heat down to a medium simmer and cook for between 20 and 30 minutes. To test for doneness, insert a fork into one of the potatoes that's on top; it should be cooked but not mushy.

Serves 4

74

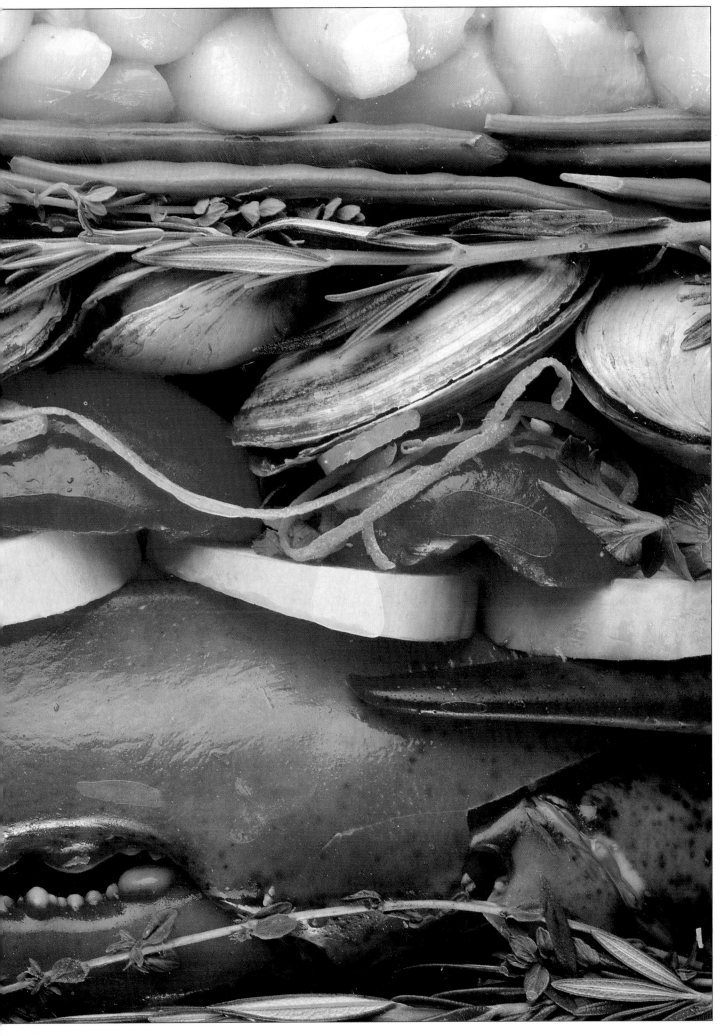

CRANBERRIES

Where the water mingles with the land in the bogs of what is now called Massachusetts, the giant Maushop and his sister Granny Squannit, the old woman of the marsh, lived, according to Wampanoag Native American legend. Granny Squannit cut her finger and the great waters of the swamp flowed out through her. She cried out, "Brother, help me. Soon I will be no more." Rushing to her aid, the lumbering giant of flesh and blood pricked his own finger to stop the wound with his vital healing fluid. As he reached over to his sister, in his haste he let a drop of blood fall, and carried by the winds, it landed among the cattails. As the second drop of blood sealed Granny Squannit's cut, the first cranberry was already arising from the giant Waushop's first wayward drop.

As befits the legend, cranberries (*Vaccinium macrocarpon*) are as exclusively native to North America as the Native Americans who greeted the Pilgrims. By the time the *Mayflower* landed, the Wampanoags and other Native Americans were using the berries in pemmican, a deer-meat precursor to beef jerky; for poultices; and as a cloth dye. The Leni-Lenape called the cranberry *ibimi*, or bitter berry, an apter description than cranberry or "crane berry," which derives from Low German and somewhat describes the pinkish-white blossoms that arch like the head of a crane.

Contrary to tradition, cranberries were probably absent from the first Thanksgiving table; cane sugar and molasses had not yet traveled up the coast, and frugality dictated that maple sugar be used on nourishing foods that required only a little sweetener. As the Pilgrims settled the land and became more assured of a ready supply of food, they began to develop recipes based on favorite dishes from home. Cranberries, for instance, served as the main ingredient in mock cherry pie. Even then, the tartness reigned. One colonial cookbook cautioned its readers: "add just so much sugar as shall leave a smart."

Thoreau called them "small waxen gems, pendants of the meadow grass, pearly and red." They were regulated by law as early as the 1770s. And they now account for almost $100 million worth of business in Massachusetts alone, the top cranberry-producing state in the United States. Although they are not as valuable as gemstones, these waxen gems have been called "red gold." As with the ore rushes of the West, the story of cranberry cultivation owes a lot to luck and observation. An alert Cape Codder noticed that the wild cranberries flourished after wind-blown sand invaded the bogs. Intentional sanding produced the same results, and so began the cranberry industry.

The cranberry lasts for a long time before spoiling, and like limes, was useful for preventing scurvy on sailing vessels and whaling ships. Today the berries appear at harvest time (September to December) and disappear from stores soon after. Nevertheless, cranberries are good all year round in bread and muffins, as relish and sauce bases, and in pies. They freeze readily if double-wrapped in plastic and last for up to nine months (don't wash them before freezing). Then just pop them into a recipe as if they were fresh (don't thaw them first).

Cranberry Apple Crisp

5 cups sliced tart apples (about 6 medium apples), stored in a bowl of water combined with the juice of one lemon to prevent discoloration

1 1/2 cups cranberries (fresh or frozen)

1/3 cup granulated sugar

1/2 cup all-purpose flour

1/2 cup brown sugar

1 teaspoon cinnamon

1/4 cup butter or margarine

Preheat oven to 375°F. Lightly grease a 9-inch square baking pan. Strain apples and if necessary pat dry. Place a layer of apples on the bottom of the pan, then put down a layer of cranberries. Sprinkle with the granulated sugar, then repeat the layering process. In a medium bowl, mix together the flour, brown sugar, and cinnamon. Cut in butter until light and crumbly. Sprinkle the brown sugar topping evenly over the fruit. Bake 45 minutes, until the apples are tender.

Serves 9

Fresh Cranberry Relish

1 pound fresh cranberries

1 apple, cored and quartered

1 orange, washed, quartered, and seeded

1 fennel bulb plus 3 stalks

6 tablespoons orange marmalade

3 tablespoons honey

1/2 cup chopped walnuts

In a food processor, grind cranberries, apple, orange, and fennel coarsely. Put mixture in a large bowl and stir in the marmalade, honey, and walnuts until well mixed. Refrigerate until serving time.

Yields 10 servings

77

78

FOODS

VERMONT'S COMMON CRACKERS

"No maid was ever filled/No manhood got enough," wrote Vermont folk poet Daniel Cady of the Vermont Common Cracker. Unsalted, hard, yet a tad flaky, Montpelier biscuits—as they are also called—resemble small, puffed, cracker-like versions of English muffins with a taste like that of thick English water biscuits. Their dryness has engendered many tales of whistling matches. Whoever whistles first after eating a plain cracker wins the bet. Split in two, however, the crackers are delicious foils for any number of moist combinations. The simplest weds two Vermont culinary classics: the common cracker and a slab of Vermont cheddar. They're also delicious toasted with a pat of butter, but true Green Mountain State tradition dictates plunging the crackers into ice water for a minute or so and letting them dry before buttering them and sticking them in the oven to puff up.

Brothers Timothy and Charles Cross baked the first common cracker in Montpelier in 1928 and set about marketing their new products by horse and wagon. Vrest Orton, the owner of the Vermont Country Store and the man who revived the baking process, remembers his family buying a barrel of crackers each year. The 1,200 crackers topped chowders and oyster stew and went into the makings for fried chicken, meatloaf, oyster stuffing, and pie crusts as well as crackers and milk. If nostalgia could be mixed into a dough and baked, it might very well take the shape of a Vermont Common Cracker.

A country store looked bare without its cracker barrel, which often revealed the character of storekeeper and customer. Less frugal storekeepers kept the barrel cover loose, an invitation for anyone to dip in and help himself. A tight cover indicated a tight personality. Greediness and frugality were also noted among customers. In fact, Vermont historian Weston Cate went so far as to state that "the cracker barrel was the center of country store life…. Indeed, the cracker barrel added a term to the language and became synonymous with informal discussions and idle talk."

The cracker almost disappeared, but with the help of Vrest Orton, it is making its way back into Vermont life as assuredly as are woodburning stoves. The Orton family bought the essential equipment and in 1981 began producing the traditional crackers. The Orton store in Weston stands as a monument to Vermont tradition. Not only can you sample the famous crackers most days, but you can find an assortment of goods ranging from flannel nightgowns and warm slippers to fiddlehead ferns, from hardware gadgets to bag balm for cows. The store remains as classic as the crackers.

© Robert Lima/Envision

Oyster Stuffing

4 cups cracker crumbs

1 pint shucked oysters, including liquor

2 onions, chopped

1 stalk celery, chopped

1/2 cup butter

1/4 cup minced parsley

1/4 teaspoon thyme

2 teaspoons lemon juice

1 teaspoon grated lemon rind

Salt and pepper to taste

Drain the oysters, reserving the liquor, and chop them. Mix the oysters together with the cracker crumbs and set aside. Sauté the onions and celery until the onions are soft and translucent, not brown. Add the onions, parsley, thyme, lemon juice, and rind to the cracker mixture, and mix well. Add approximately 1/4 cup of the reserved liquor to moisten the mixture. Season to taste with salt and pepper. Bake at 325°F for 30 minutes.

NEW ENGLAND CRAFTS & COLLECTIBLES

The line between fine art and folk art is a
blurry one that is repeatedly fine-tuned and
focused, as binoculars are, for each person.
The line between crafts and folk art is equally
vague. Scholars argue back and forth debating
the merits of, on one hand connoisseurship, and
on the other, sociology. It's the old "one is art,
the other, furniture" debate. Does a folk art
object have intrinsic artistic worth when it's
separated from its context? Leave the worrying
to the historians; just appreciate the skill or
imagination that infuses each work.

Stephen Huneck, an artist by preference,
illustrates a fine example of the partitions that

the art world imposes on its denizens. Huneck trained himself as a woodworker, repairing and restoring antiques, a trade that eventually led him to try his hand at carving wood as an art. His weathervane-like carvings, unlike any others, caused a stir in the antiques business. His vision was good enough to rouse people's passions and his skill so great that Huneck inadvertently fooled more than one dealer into thinking he had a genuinely old article. His current work not only reaches into the past but also examines the present and anticipates the future.

The separations in this book parallel those of the art world at large. Discussions of baskets, scrimshaw, and weathervanes could fall under either crafts and folk art or collectibles, so please excuse the arbitrariness of the decisions, and instead enjoy the stories that so often accompany an artist's rendering of his world.

To balance out the more complicated arts that require more skill and training, there is a trio of kitchen crafts designed for beginners. Rooted in the routines of a Colonial kitchen, these crafts should be shared with children of all ages.

Shelburne Museum, Shelburne, Vermont

*T*he exact origin of the Nantucket light-ship basket (page 82) lies obscured in history, but Native American designs surely were influential. New England china is a popular collectible (page 84). The work of Steve Huneck (this page) reflects modern craft ideas.

CRAFTS AND COLLECTIBLES

"It is art that makes life, makes interest, makes importance, for our consideration and application of these things, and I know of no substitute whatever for the force and beauty of its process."
—*Henry James,* from a letter to H.G. Wells, July 10, 1915

Few know the details of the theft, but the famous—many authorities say the *most* famous—American weathervane, the grasshopper atop Boston's Fanueil Hall, disappeared one night in the winter of 1974. The noble, gilt creature—an interpreted copy of the vane atop London's Royal Exchange—had survived a fire, an earthquake, the Boston Massacre, even the vagaries of celebrations; it remained in one piece despite surgery done to its legs and antennae; yet under cover of dark, the 52-inch giant hopped its perch after 232 years. The papers reported the loss at once, and an investigation began immediately; little did the thief realize that his masterpiece was almost as illustrious as the *Winged Victory.* With no buyer wanting a "hot" property, the burglar abandoned his treasure where he had left it: in the attic of the Hall. The Fanueil Hall grasshopper was remounted, and to this day it looks out over the city and the harbor.

The theft, no doubt, was spurred on by auction prices for weathervanes in the early seventies that topped $10,000. By 1989, the *New York Times* reported that the price for at least one vane, a locomotive, had risen above $200,000 and that weathervanes had gained respectability. Weathervanes are no longer considered quaint artifacts. They are, rather, steadfast fellows of American folk sculpture.

The word *vane* comes from Old English "fana," meaning a banner or flag. Over the centuries wood or metal eventually replaced cloth; and legions of barnyard animals or other close-to-home motifs displaced initials and coats of arms. In America, the vanes represented a new equality: Anyone could erect a metal banner to fly in the face of the wind. Not only did people from all walks of life brandish a vane, but they let very little limit their imagination.

Rooftops boasted goddesses of liberty, angels, cherubs, centaurs, and mermaids, as well as pigs, cows, bulls, ewes, and ubiquitous roosters. Horses came with buggies, sulkies, jockeys, unidentified riders, and grooms. They pranced, reared, ran, trotted, and jumped through rings. Whales, dolphins, square-rigged ships, swordfish, and cod beautified seaside towns, while squirrels, stags, eagles, and game birds adorned inland villages. Their inspiration was personal or practical, as varied as the images themselves.

The cock, for instance, heralded its call from many a church steeple, some say because it represented the dutiful cockerel that roused Peter's conscience after he denied Jesus. It soon lost its religious significance and gained a new reputation as a proud surveyor of a man's land. One of the better books on vanes, *A Gallery of American Weathervanes and Whirligigs,* quotes Pablo Picasso on the chanticleer: "Cocks, there have always been cocks, but like everything else in life we must discover them—just as Corot discovered the morning and Renoir discovered girls.... Cocks have always been seen, but never as well as in American weathervanes." In contrast to the everyday-made-special is the special-made-extraordinary, as with the 48-inch pine elephant that hails from Bridgeport, Connecticut, the home of huckster and circus impresario P.T. Barnum. The 1880 prize probably depicts Jumbo, one of Barnum's performing mammoths.

The symbols and figures of weathervanes, made to be seen from many feet below, seem small from the ground, when in truth some are as large as a small person. Some are of wood and others are of metal; some appear in silhouette and others were crafted three-dimensionally. Artisans handcrafted the early vanes, chiseling or

Shelburne Museum, Shelburne, Vermont

Even though an antique vane may be pitted and scored, it is precisely these imperfections in the original finish that make it valuable. Design comes into play, too, and this Indian vane from the Shelburne Museum is one of the more intriguing classic styles.

87

Craftspeople today who make real weathervanes, the kind that stand up to forty-mile-an-hour gusts, are few and far between. As folk art has gained respectability, weathervanes are taking up space inside the home and being pampered by feather dusters. And for good reason: the shapes capture a readiness to take on the elements, to stand up to the worst that nature can dole out, and that brings drama to interior design schemes.

But of course, not everyone can afford to buy expensive weathervanes. A good alternative is to copy the shapes of the classic weathervanes onto more accessible surfaces—like notepaper for greeting cards, or onto cloth that you plan to embroider, or even onto thin sheet metal which you've cut with tin snips.

Here are some traditional weathervane designs which you can enlarge and trace onto whatever surface you wish (some people have even been known to use them for stenciling borders along walls and cabinets).

When using the patterns included here, keep in mind these simple hints for enlarging or reducing the design:

1) Use a ruler or triangle to get right angles in the corners.

2) Start with a piece of paper big enough to accommodate both the enlarged figure and a tracing of the original figure.

3) Trace the figure onto the upper lefthand corner of the paper, then draw a box to enclose it .

4) Extend the righthand vertical border down the page; extend the bottom horizontal border across the page to the right.

5) Draw a diagonal line from the upper lefthand corner of the traced figure's box to the bottom righthand corner of the box and extend it down the page.

6) Construct a square that will enclose the enlarged figure (the dimensions will vary according to your needs). If you've made proper right angles, the diagonal line from the upper lefthand corner of the traced figure's square should neatly go through the bottom righthand corner of the square just completed.

7) In this step, you're basically making your own graph paper. Mark the sides of each square in even increments (eighths, sixteenths, etc.), and mark rules on the paper. Use more divisions for more complex designs.

8) Where each line of the design intersects a graphed line, mark a dot on the original design and on the grid where you will draw the enlarged design. Using the dots as aids, draw the design in.

9) Cut the shape out and use it as a decorating pattern.

pounding away, creating one-of-a-kind artifacts. But by the mid-nineteenth century almost all vanes came from a factory mold. Surprisingly, the factory vanes often command as good a price as handmade versions that may be in poorer condition. Very few seventeenth- and eighteenth-century weathervanes exist, so collectors have turned to the notable manufacturers such as J. Harris & Company of Boston; J. Howard & Company of West Bridgewater, Massachusetts;

...ple of how a graph can be
...to transfer and enlarge a
...ervane design.

A. L. Jewell & Company, Cushing and White, and L. W. Cushing & Sons, all of Waltham, Massachusetts; Chelmsford Foundry Company of Chelmsford, Massachusetts; and Rochester Iron Works of Rochester, New Hampshire.

Even the production vanes required an artist's hand to generate fine details and graceful stances. What began as a sketch turned first to a clay model then to a negative plaster cast and later to a reverse plaster cast. The two plaster halves fit to form the whole figure. The plaster casts then became the master for an iron mold into which the craftsman worked a large sheet of copper, forming and shaping the pliable metal with specialized hammers. A blanket of lead drove the copper farther into the iron mold. The definition—of eyes, hair, or mouths—was left to be done by hand. The final step of joining the two completed copper halves was done simply by soldering.

President John F. Kennedy collected scrimshaw and influenced an entire generation of whalebone enthusiasts. Today's market is extremely variable. Scrimshander David Lazarus says, "A good antique piece may cost anywhere from $2,000 to $22,000" depending on the quality and condition of the piece. "Similarly, a contemporary piece could be a $40 piece of jewelry or an $8,000 jawbone." These pictures illustrate the diversity within the craft.

SCRIMSHAW

Eight great species of whales dominated the world's oceans in the 1700s when seamen from Nantucket left their home island to establish the American whaling industry. Sailing ships plied the waters from the North Atlantic to Patagonia and beyond, and as they often spent over a year at sea, the men aboard whiled away their time doodling on the nearest available raw material: whale bone and sperm-whale teeth. Scrimshaw, the result of this doodling, is loosely defined as the art of carving or engraving on whalebone and whale ivory, as the teeth are called, although the definition now extends to similar skilled work on surfaces as varied as walrus ivory, fossil mammoth tusk, and Corian, a new-age plastic.

Whaling decimated the marine mammal's legendary numbers. The great animals that once were common on the high seas have all become endangered; pitifully few remain. Scientists count fewer than one hundred individuals for some species, and even that number may not be enough to hold off extinction. The scientific community doesn't yet know how many whales must survive to maintain a viable gene pool for a healthy, continuing population. And despite an outcry to stop the killing, the slaughter continues by some nations under the guise of research. The United States, however, has placed a moratorium on whaling, and thanks to the Marine Mammal Act of 1972 and the Endangered Species Act of 1973, whale imports are banned and interstate commerce of whale goods—including scrimshaw—is restricted.

Scrimshaw really falls into two if not three categories: old scrimshaw and new scrimshaw, and imitation old scrimshaw. The "old scrimshaw," writes scrimshander and author William Gilkerson, "was an escape from the sea—from too much sea—back towards the land. The new scrimshaw moves in the other direction." The old scrimshaw is a national treasure, a folk art of great charm that peaked between 1825 and 1875. Sailors etched scenes and figures from their surroundings, from magazines, and from their imagination, saving in ivory images of hula dancers, Indian princesses, angels, wives, sweethearts, mermaids, Justice, and Liberty as well as eagles, florals, coats of arms, sea battles, and proud ships. When home, the objects—corset busks, knitting needles, pie crimpers, and the like—became favored artifacts, to be looked at rather than used.

CRAFTS AND COLLECTIBLES

*I*ntricate scrimshaw work kept sailors busy during long months at sea. Beautiful objects such as these (page 93) resulted from their labors.

The new scrimshaw focuses more on the artist's skill and less on the surface material. "Today, people really should consider that the artwork of a scrimshander is paramount, more important than the materials on which they engrave," says David Lazarus, an English-born Nantucket scrimshander. Lazarus came to the craft after a career illustrating books. "The subject matter I prefer to portray has a lot to do with public feeling. Obviously, we [contemporary scrimshanders] don't portray so many pictures of the whale being dispatched or harpooned. We prefer to show the whale upsetting the boat. There is a definite move toward showing the survival of the species rather than its demise." Lazarus pioneered scrimshawing on new plastics like Corian, and for beginners he suggests turning to old Formica as a practice surface. As each old scrimshander had his preference for tools and dyes, so does each new scrimshander. Lazarus highlights his pictures with oil paints; Gilkerson, with India ink; the old sailors, lampblack mixed with spit or oil. Lazarus recommends a sail needle for beginners; Gilkerson, an X-Acto knife. As for the old sailors: "With gimlets and awls they bored and pierced holes; with needles and knives they pricked and incised designs," wrote Celia Oliver and Robert Shaw in *An American Sampler: Folk Art from the Shelburne Museum*. Smoothing and finishing, then as now is left to sandpaper, although some sailors used sharkskin for the final touch.

How many scrimshanders are still working? "Fewer and fewer by the day," says Lazarus; "I think a lot of us are hanging up the old tools."

SCRIMSHAW 101

Materials needed:

Old Formica (scrap from countertops, for example)

Sail needle or artist's knife

Pencil

India ink or oil paint (optional)

Fine brush (optional)

Fine sandpaper

Directions:

These instructions give you an introduction to what scrimshawing is like:

1) Start by cutting the Formica into small sections. (A sperm whale's panbone, part of the back jawbone, is one of the largest surfaces a scrimshander had to work with. A typical rectangle carved from the bone might measure about $6^1/_2$ inches by $10^1/_2$ inches. A tooth usually stands about $5^1/_2$ to $7^1/_2$ inches high. In contrast, a long, thin tusk measures approximately $13^1/_2$ inches by $1^1/_2$ inches.)

2) Either scratch in the design freehand with the sail needle, or draw it in lightly with a pencil first and then scratch it in.

3) Smooth the edges with sandpaper.

4) Darken the design with ink or paint, let dry, and if necessary, sand again.

CRAFTS AND COLLECTIBLES

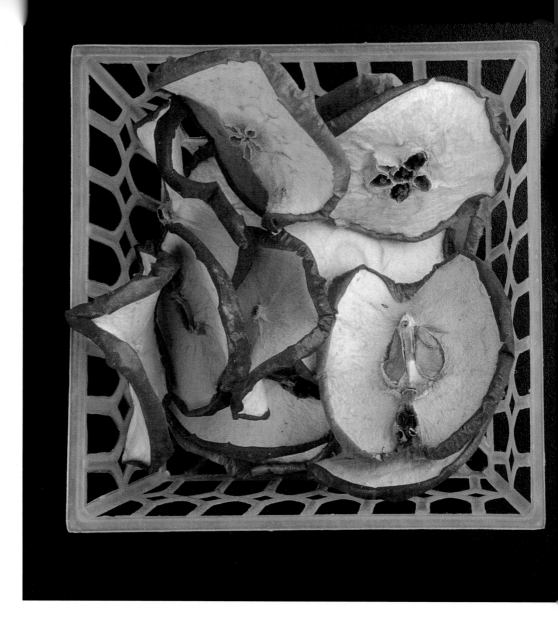

KITCHEN CRAFTS

Many of the simpler crafts in New England originated in the kitchen and used products of the land. It's easy to conjure up a toasty kitchen, heated by a fire or woodstove, with baskets and food hanging from the rafters, dogs curled up in the corner, and the woman of the house resting in a rocking chair, probably knitting. But reality, as it so often does, can dash the romance from this idyllic picture. One early New England colonist described her kitchen in winter as being so cold that while the fire warmed her backside, ice froze in a cup she held in front of her. Yet, despite the hardships and the long hours toiling, women often found time to create what we now call artifacts, some useful, others purely decorative. The kitchen crafts described below are updated ver-sions of what a Colonial housewife might have made.

As Louisa May Alcott wrote in *An Old-Fashioned Thanksgiving*, "The big kitchen was a jolly place just now, for in the great fire-place roared a cheerful fire; on the wall hung garlands of dried apples, onions, and corn; up aloft from the beams shone crook-necked squashes, juicy hams, and dried venison…" The cornhusk doll, dried apple wreath, and gourd ornament probably would have been a welcome addition to an early New England home.

DRIED APPLE WREATH

The Pilgrims carried apple seeds and cuttings with them on the *Mayflower*, and this remarkable fruit that's kin to

Greening and Romes following behind. It doesn't matter what apple you use to make the wreath, which is so simple that a child can do the stringing. Instead of having dried apples hanging from the rafters, put together this miniature wreath.

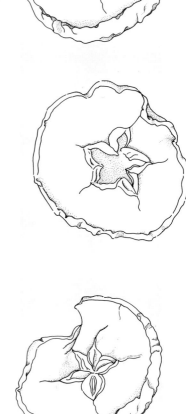

Materials:

Approximately 5 apples

Mixing bowl filled with cold water and $1/2$ cup lemon juice

Gas oven

Colander

Cookie sheets

Two feet of festive ribbon

Large-eyed blunt needle

Paper clip

Directions:

1) Slice the fruit into $1/4$- to $1/2$-inch rounds using a stainless-steel knife. Be careful as you cut through the core, as it will offer resistance. Plunge the slices into the water as you cut them, and put them in a colander immediately to dry. Pat dry.

2) Place the slices on a cookie sheet in a single layer. Put them in the oven with the heat off (the pilot light will keep it warm) for about 4 days. If you want to use the oven during this period, take the apple slices out first, then let it cool down before you put them back in to dry. Repeat this process until you have about 60 slices. The apples will be hard and shriveled but interestingly shaped.

3) Thread the needle with the ribbon and weave the slices together. Unthread the needle, and tie a big bow.

4) Slip the paper clip in under the apples for a hook.

the rose took to the New England climate heartily. By the middle of the eighteenth century, Yankees were already exporting apples to the Caribbean.

There's nothing quite like apple picking when the air turns brisk in New England. All the New England states grow apples, but Massachusetts gave birth to Johnny Appleseed (born John Chapman in either Leominster or Springfield). Perhaps he was influenced by the hill country between the Berkshires and the Connecticut River where apple orchards give way to breathtaking views.

The first pickings of the season are most likely to be sweet Red Delicious and the more tart McIntosh, with winter apples such as Rhode Island

© Tim Gibson/Envision

GOURD ORNAMENT

I've heard of native New Englanders who ignore the blend of color and light that make foliage season so spectacular. I've even met a few. But, like electricity and quarks, I find these people mysteries of science. (Then again, one year when the Midwest conspired to keep me away from home during leaf season, I cadged a cold and windy twenty-two-hour ride in the back of an open pickup to get to New England, only to turn around after a four-hour hike and a quick shower.)

New England autumns are oxymorons: Timeless anachronisms, they weave nostalgia into current life in such a way that neither is complete without the other. New England autumns are details. They are the sheaves of wheat leaning against suburban lampposts. They are the damp, earthy smells from leaves no longer waiting to be burned, leaves still piled in mounds waiting only to be jumped in. They are the farmstands with baskets of gourds so plentiful and so varied they seem like ornaments to be hung on the fall trees, which sometimes seem more deserving than the evergreens of Christmas.

Orange, white, green, and yellow. Thin stripes, wide bands. It doesn't take much to recast these members of the family *Cucurbitaceae* into baubles. Colonists fashioned them into bowls and dairy skimmers, cups, bottles, and grain holders. Their handsomeness complemented their usefulness.

The following directions are beginner's instructions. These basics can be adapted to almost any gourd.

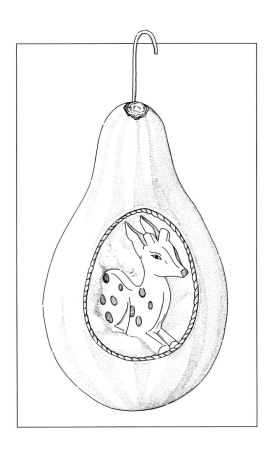

Materials:

A small orange-and-white striped gourd

Soapless, fine steel wool

Craft knife

Fine sandpaper

White glue

Cotton swabs

Cotton balls

Scrap of trim (eyelet lace, gold ribbon, etc.)

Clear wax or clear acrylic artist's spray paint

Small paper clip

Small length of florist's tape

Miniature porcelain animal or figurine

Directions:

1) Choose an unblemished gourd that appeals to you. Wash it, pat dry, then wipe with a solution of 1 part vinegar to 1 part water. Set the gourd out of the way to dry (this may take several days).

2) Etch a cutting line into the gourd. (Handle the gourd as if it were a delicate Christmas ornament; the dried skin becomes brittle and can break easily.) With the crafts knife, cut the circle out gently. Then scrape away the seeds and flesh from the interior. Rinse and pat dry.

3) If you have a gas oven, place it in the oven with the heat turned off (the pilot will keep it warm) for an hour. Or, preheat an electric oven to 200° F, then turn it off and put the gourd inside for an hour.

4) Lightly sand the edges of the cutting line.

5) Using the cotton swabs, apply a thin layer of glue to the inside of the gourd. Press on a single layer of cotton balls. Repeat this process until the entire interior of the gourd is lined with cotton.

6) Cut a length of trim to cover the circumference of the edge of the hole. Glue the trim on so that it fits over the interior and exterior edge, giving the hole a finished appearance.

7) With the tip of the knife, prick a hole into the top of the gourd. Insert a small paper clip into this hole. Bend the clip into an ornament hook, then cover with florist's tape or extra trim.

8) Apply two coats of wax or spray paint to the outside.

9) Finally, position a small porcelain collectible inside the ornament and glue in place.

BAYBERRY CANDLES

When the colonists first settled in America and tallow from cattle was scarce, the colonists burned split pitch pine—or candlewood—even though it produced a thick smoke and tarry drippings. "It was said that a prudent New England farmer would as soon start the winter without hay in his barn as without candle-wood in his shed," wrote Alice Morse Earle in 1898 in *Home Life in Colonial Days*. The pitch pine worked best by the fireplace where the smoke could take advantage of the chimney. Candles, a more precious commodity, lit the remainder of the house.

To make the candles, the settlers turned to deer suet, moose fat, and bear's grease for ingredients, then to bee's wax once they established hives. The bayberry *(Myrica pensylvanica)*, which ripens in the autumn, became a much-sought-after alternative, for the candles made from their wax burned better than common tallow and in addition gave off a sweet smell. Bayberry candles were, in fact, the first scented candles to be made by the colonists.

One traveler to the United States in 1748, Swedish naturalist Professor Kalm, wrote that the pea-sized bayberry looked "as if flour had been strewed on them." He noted that "candles of this do not easily bend, nor melt in summer as common candles do; they burn better and slower, nor do they cause any smoke...."

Whaling introduced expensive whale oil and assorted lamps to burn it, in place of candles, but the settlers continued to make bayberry and tallow candles regularly well into the 1800s, when they finally were eclipsed by kerosene, gas, oil, and then electricity.

The history of candlemaking found a new home in western Massachusetts at the end of 1989 when Yankee Candle Company opened The Yankee Candlemaking Museum, in Deerfield, "the only candlemaking museum in the United States and one of the few in the world," says director Carol Griffin. Owner Michael Kittridge began making hand-dipped tapers in his parents' home at the age of 17. As the company grew, so did his collection of related artifacts, many of which the museum has on display, including a rare part-wood, part-tin candle mold made by the J. Walker Company of Bloomfield, Connecticut, circa 1810.

Unlike the company, the museum store does not have a mail-order service, but they do sell unusual, custom-made candle molds, kettles for candle making, and bayberry candles made the old-fashioned way. For candle-making kits with dyed and scented wax and wicks and for blocks of paraffin—both with instructions on how to make dipped and molded candles—write directly to the company: Yankee Candle Company, Route 5, South Deerfield, Massachusetts 01373. Both the factory and the museum welcome visitors, and the company has retail stores throughout New England.

Here's how the colonists made bayberry candles. You probably won't want to try this recipe, for two reasons. One, you'd have to go out and pick for hours to get enough bayberries. And two, these directions call for setting the berries on a woodstove all night long. Not that many people these days keep their stoves burning all night, and those that do probably don't want to risk the fire that might ensue from leaving wax melting unattended. But these instructions give a clear picture of how New Englanders made candles back when they depended on them for light.

An Old-Fashioned Recipe for Bayberry Candle Wax

10 pounds bayberries

Colander and sieve

Heavy pot or kettle large enough to hold the berries and water

Cheesecloth

© Christopher Bain

To make candle wax the old-fashioned way, gather together or buy approximately 10 pounds of bayberries. Sort through the berries, removing any traces of leaves and twigs. In batches, fill a colander with berries and shake the colander back and forth to eliminate any dust. Fill a large pot or kettle with the berries as you finish "dusting" them, then fill the pot with water, leaving a few inches of water at the top. On a woodstove, put the pot in the middle of the stove away from direct heat. Avoid direct heat as it will cause sediment to mix into the wax. Leave the pot overnight, then remove to a cold place, preferably out of doors, for the entire day. The wax will form into a cohesive solid.

Take the wax from the pot and remove any sediment from its surface, brushing lightly if necessary. Fill a heavy kettle with water, then add the wax. Set the kettle on top of the woodstove (again, avoid direct heat) until melted. Strain the warm wax through a sieve, then through clean cheesecloth. If the wax still has impurities, cool it outside, then repeat the melting and straining process. (If you do the straining near the stove, be careful not to spill the wax or burn yourself on the stove.) By now the wax should have changed from a dirty green to a clear green color. Place the warm, strained wax in a clean, old teapot or pitcher for easy handling. Then make your candles with molds, or by dipping.

Yields 1 pound wax

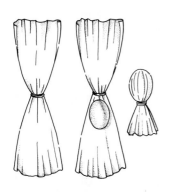

4 & 5

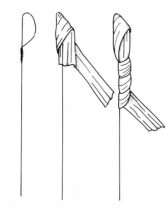

100

7

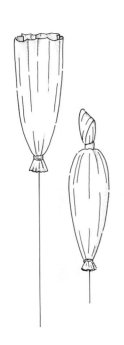

8

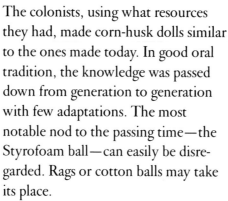

© Robert Perron

CORNHUSK DOLL

The colonists, using what resources they had, made corn-husk dolls similar to the ones made today. In good oral tradition, the knowledge was passed down from generation to generation with few adaptations. The most notable nod to the passing time—the Styrofoam ball—can easily be disregarded. Rags or cotton balls may take its place.

As with most simple crafts, the artisan always leaves his or her mark on the object, intentionally or not. The basic doll described below is a jumping-off point. From there you can incorporate shawls, brooms, baskets, bonnets, or aprons—whatever comes to mind from the material—into plans for a more elaborate doll.

Materials:

Cornhusks

Cornsilk, unspun wool, or flax

Newspapers

Old terry-cloth towel

Heavyweight white or light-colored cotton thread

1-inch Styrofoam ball

15 inches of medium-weight wire

Cotton balls

Scissors

White glue

Directions:

1) To prepare your own husks (rather than buying them prepared), first shuck the corn, sorting out the coarser outer husks from the fine-grained inner husks and setting aside the corn silk for the doll's hair. Place the husks and silk between two newspapers and let them dry in a warm, dry place for about a week.

2) Whether you buy or dry the husks, when you're ready to make the doll, you'll want to soak the husks in water for between 5 and 10 minutes to make them supple and easy to work with. Don't soak them too long or they will discolor. Then lay them out on a dampened, wrung-out towel. Fold the towel over or place another dampened towel on top to keep the husks moist while you make the doll.

3) Square off the ends of a fine-grained husk that's approximately 3 inches wide.

4) With the smoother side to the outside, tie a length of thread around the middle of the husk and wind the thread around the husk a few turns before knotting it on the inside. Place the Styrofoam ball just under the thread and wrap the husk snugly around the ball, tying both ends on the opposite side of the ball from the thread.

5) Wind more thread around the bottom of the loose ends of the husk at the base of the wrapped ball to form the neck. The husks below the neck will supplement the body.

6) Snip a 6- or 7-inch length of wire and push it up into the neck and head for support. Set aside.

7) For the arms, snip a 9-inch length of wire and make a small loop at either end for the hands. Cut a few $^2/_3$-inch strips from a husk to cover the loops and partially cover the wire arms. Wrap as if you were using florist's wire. Secure the husks by tying a bit of thread around the doll's "wrists."

8) Cut two husks to measure 3 inches by 5 inches for sleeves. Work one arm at a time. Tie the husk onto the wrist tightly so that the length of the husk extends out away from the center of the doll. Turn the husk inside out, forming the gathered full sleeve. Tie the husk to the top of the arm, which should be approximately in the center of the wire.

9) Join the head to the arms by pushing the extending head wire through the center of the arms. Tie with thread to secure.

10) For the torso, gather cotton balls into a ball approximately 2$^1/_2$ inches across. Cut a husk to measure 3 inches by 5 inches and place the cotton balls in the center. Fold the husk over and tie with thread, making the doll's waist. Insert the connecting wire into the newly made torso. Lace a thread over the doll's shoulders, crisscrossing in front, and tie it around the waist.

10

11) The blouse will require two husks cut to measure 2 inches by 5 inches. Centering the first husk on one shoulder, crisscross it like a sash over the doll's torso; do the same for the other shoulder; then tie them in place with more thread at the waist.

12) To make the skirt, choose eight wide husks (they should measure at least 7 or 8 inches across) and place them around the doll's waist so that the husks—wider ends out—extend above the doll rather than below it. Secure the husks at the waist with thread, then turn them down to form a full skirt. Trim the hem of the skirt evenly. Tie a thread—or a scrap of material—loosely around the skirt so that it keeps the shape without binding the husks.

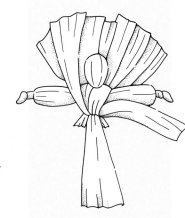

12

13) Make sure the doll's arms are in place as you want them. Use the glue to close any gaps in the arms or in the skirt, then let the doll dry for two days. Snip the string.

14) Make hair from corn silk, wool, or flax by tying it together and then gluing it onto the doll's head.

14

101

Shelburne Museum, Shelburne, Vermont

become familiar with the companies and individuals who produced the finest examples of a particular collectible. Get to know the markings—whether they are names, monograms, or symbols—that distinguish one company or individual from another and special features that are unique to the pieces you are collecting, so that you will be able to tell the difference between genuine articles and reproductions. Even if you are building a collection of contemporary objects, it's helpful to learn the history of their medium so that you will be able to recognize quality items when you see them.

Most people become engrossed with collecting a specific category and assembling a particular type of variation within it. For example, some people exclusively collect Bennington pottery. You may wish to start off by collecting a wide range of examples of one medium and gradually begin to focus on particular pieces that you find appealing. Craftsmanship is a tradition in New England, and many of the items that we think of as collectible today were originally made as utilitarian objects for around the home. As the colonies prospered and there was more time for leisurely pursuits, including an appreciation of beautiful, handmade objects, a greater emphasis on the artistic merits of items grew, and their creators developed their skills accordingly. Some of the most interesting private collections recognize and catalog this chronology within a medium. A collector's knowledge of how a particular form developed —whether the medium is glass or basketry—helps train the eye to detect and appreciate those subtle touches that distinguish well-made items from art.

Whether you admire the disarming charm of scrimshaw folk art or the virtuoso craftsmanship of handmade glass, there are limitless possibilities for beginning a collection of objects that are unique to New England. For the contemporary connoisseur of New England goods, the challenge is to build an interesting and varied collection, while also finding the proper way to display and protect these treasures. This is particularly important with glass and pottery, which demand to be displayed yet are so fragile that they must be protected from damage, perhaps in a glass case or high on a shelf out of harm's way.

To build a collection and give yourself a direction in which to head, it's valuable to give yourself a background in the history of the particular art form you admire. Through reading up on the subject and visiting museums, you will

Shelburne Museum, Shelburne, Vermont

*B*ennington Pottery
was produced in
abundance and col-
lected avidly by New
Englanders during the
eighteenth and nine-
teenth centuries (this
page, top). The details
of lacy pressed Sand-
wich glass from the
Victorian era are
impressive (this page,
bottom). Scrimshaw
takes many forms
(page 102).

103

Courtesy of The Sandwich Historical Society/Glass Museum

The components of a Nantucket light-ship basket (this page) owe much to sailing coopers (basketmakers) who named the parts after the parts of boats. The basket's vertical splints are called staves, *the bottom rounds* bottoms, *and the top binding* hoops. *The sailors honed their skills, and the best constructed eight baskets that nested one inside the other (page 105) which ranged from pint-size to twelve-quart capacity. Artisans now make small sets of nesting baskets in gold as collector's items and jewelry.*

104

Courtesy of Four Winds Craft Guild, Nantucket, photograph © Jack Weinhold

Baskets

Route 91, near Putney, Vermont, used to have many signs advertising a wonderful old shop called Basketville.

While the signs may not be as ubiquitous, Basketville continues to make and sell new products. And the market for old, handmade New England baskets has skyrocketed. Although it's still possible to find nineteenth-century examples of Yankee basketry for under $25 at a tag sale, it's just as likely that a piece in good condition with provenance will sell at auction for over $1,000. Most baskets, however, fall in between in price and end up for sale at knowledgeable dealers.

Basketry is considered by many scholars to be the oldest craft in the world, with American baskets dating back 9,000 years (found in a cave in Utah), so it is no surprise that when the Europeans first came to the New World they found Native Americans already producing well-wrought containers of woven plant fibers. In New England, the Iroquois and members of the large Algonquian nation traded baskets for cloth and other European imports. In time, the settlers learned the art, but Native Americans continued to provide baskets and raw materials for baskets to the New England white community—the Shakers among them—well into the nineteenth century when factory-made baskets all but replaced the handmade goods.

Besides the Native American baskets,

New England is home to generic black-ash splint baskets, Shaker baskets, and Nantucket lightship baskets. The task for a collector lies in attempting to determine where a basket originated, for few were signed as artwork and, making it harder, many of the traditions overlapped among the separate communities. In fact, most basketry experts suggest that the only real guide to determining origin is developing a sixth sense of sorts for the shapes, materials, and workmanship of the particular type of basket you want to collect. Once you've decided that a basket fits in a certain time period in a specific region, you still may not be able to pin down its provenance. For instance, a carefully woven, simple "fancy" basket identified as Shaker could easily have been crafted by a nearby tradesman who also had a good eye and a precise hand. A typical "New England" ash splint basket may just as easily have been made by a Native American as a settler.

The black ash tree (called the brown ash in some New England areas) lends itself to basketmaking. With some pounding, the tree's growth rings naturally split into strong, continuous splints that can be split again by hand for a finer splint. The torn then smoothed splints are much sturdier than machine-cut splints that can't always follow the natural grain of the wood.

Most of the baskets found in the antique market today were handcrafted

yet woven over forms that produced baskets of the same size. Thus, baskets became measures of their day. There were oyster baskets, clam baskets, bushel baskets, and peck baskets, all standardized. Other baskets held everything from heavy potatoes to fragile berries to lightweight seeds. Inside the house, baskets carried laundry, held eggs, organized sewing notions, and drained cheese. One clever crafter even came up with a design for a narrow basket to place over a goose's head while the bird was being plucked. And some Native American baskets were so finely woven they could carry water.

The settlers were good consumers, and the Native Americans quickly ascertained what the colonists wanted. They soon began weaving baskets over forms as well. So did the Shakers.

Contrary to what many beginning collectors think, there is no one basket called a Shaker basket. The Shakers, like their "outside" counterparts, used baskets for a variety of chores, and produced an array of baskets just like other New England settlers. Gloria Roth Teleki, author of *The Baskets of Rural America* wrote: "Shaker designs were not really original with them but were simplified and refined versions of extant forms." The difference basically lies in the workmanship. Mother Ann, the spiritual leader of the Shakers, wrote: "Do your work as though you had a thousand years to live and as if you were to die tomorrow." The celibate religious sect became well-known for precision work and simplicity of design.

Collectors are especially drawn to Shaker fancy baskets, whose name in this case means not ornamental but of above-average quality. By the mid-1800s, more fancy baskets were being made for sale than utility baskets; factories could make fair-enough reproductions of utility baskets, but could not duplicate the fine work required of the smaller, more delicate

fancy baskets. Technically, these baskets originated with the Mount Lebanon, New York, Shaker community and then through the teachings of Shakers such as Sister Cornelia French, the technique spread to the Sabbathday Lake and other New England communities. All of the Shaker villages produced baskets according to their credo to aim for self-sufficiency. In New England, these included groups at Canterbury and Enfield, New Hampshire; Sabbathday Lake, Maine; and Harvard and Hancock, Massachusetts.

Another New England basket tradition—the making of Nantucket lightship baskets—is atypical in comparison to other basketry legacies. First, unlike other New England baskets, they are made with a nonnative material: imported rattan. Second, many of them are signed or otherwise marked by their makers. Third, the craft continues on the island, with some new baskets commanding almost as much attention as old ones.

Although many of the baskets now selling at auction for upward of $3,000 were made in the mid-twentieth century by craftsman Jose Reyes on Nantucket, the tradition got its start, most scholars agree, when the first South Shoal lightship was established in 1853. The lightship took the place of a lighthouse, and the sailors who manned the ship had little to do.

Grooved-wood bottoms served as bases for the oval or round baskets, which also boasted swing handles and oak uprights. It was Reyes who created the handbag basket most in demand today. He topped the open basket with a wooden lid adorned by a piece of carved ebony, ivory, or scrimshaw. Nesting baskets, usually eight to the set, also command high prices, whether they're new or old. As a final tribute to the tradition and to the artists, jewelers are now crafting the tiny lightship baskets in gold.

This cobalt blue pressed glass nappy (serving dish) fitted with a decorative cover exemplifies the virtuosity of the Sandwich glass makers.

Glass

The most beautiful, plentiful, and collectible type of New England glass is undoubtedly the art glass produced in the Victorian period. Examples from previous eras are scarce, owing to the fragility of glass. Beginning in 1920 in America, a new appreciation for historic glass gave rise to many fakes and reproductions, and collectors began to go to great lengths to verify the authenticity of particular pieces. Major excavations of old New England glassworks took place to find clues to the origins of existing pieces and possibly to find some old buried treasure. Harry Hall White commented in the June 1927 issue of *Antiques* magazine, "From the standpoint of possible discovery, the site of an old glass factory occupies in my mind relatively the same position as an old attic."

Such excavations made it possible to definitively catalog the origins of various glass pieces. There is indeed a rich variety of objects from which to choose to collect. American art glass began when Joseph Locke of the New England Glass Company of East Cambridge, Massachusetts, invented Amberina, a colored glass blown in shades from amber to ruby red in a special process. This invention spurred other glass companies, such as the Mount Washington Glass Company of New Bedford, Massachusetts, to produce similar fancy glassware under the name Rose Amber.

Ingenious methods for producing a variety of effects ensued all over New England. The New England Glass Company expanded its repertoire to produce Agata, which reproduces agate's mottled look, and Silvered Glass, a beautiful variety coated with silver nitrate.

The Boston & Sandwich Glass Company, which was founded by Deming Jarves in 1825 in Sandwich, Massachusetts, began producing Craquelle, a blown glass with a rough texture; Mary Gregory glass, a translucent colored type adorned with figures of children; Satin glass, another translucent colored form, but one that

108

might be lined with white milk glass; Threaded glass, which was ornamented with parallel lines of colored or clear glass; and Latticino glass, a type decorated with strands of undulating, interlocking glass that was embedded in the glass. Deming Jarves also began the Cape Cod Glass Works in Sandwich in 1858, and this company produced cut and pressed glass as well as Vasa Murrhina, a clear glass that was embedded with metal and small pieces of colored glass.

Elsewhere in New England, glass was made at a number of locations, although it was of a different, less extravagant aesthetic than the type produced at Sandwich. In Connecticut, the Coventry Glass Works, operating between 1831 and 1848, produced historic flasks commemorating events in American history in amber and aquamarine glass. Other popular flask types were the varieties reading "Success to the Railroad" in olive green and amber and Cornucopia-Urn and Sunburst flasks in amber. At Keene, New Hampshire, the Keene Glass Works made gorgeous aquamarine Sunburst flasks and amber Masonic and Eagle-Masonic flasks. Glassworks at Stoddard, New Hampshire made black, green and amber ware and produced "flag flasks" in olive amber, sporting the American flag, as well as the large pitchers with

a superimposed lily-pad decoration, which are avidly sought by contemporary collectors.

Pottery

Pottery was once a thriving business in New England, although not all items that were sold there were locally made. It wasn't until the late eighteenth and nineteenth centuries, however, that the local craft came to be truly appreciated by New Englanders. Before this time, the trade was dominated by China and England. Pottery collectors should take note that in the late eighteenth century after the American Revolution, many British potters betrayed their homeland by producing items with an American nationalistic theme. So if you come upon pottery bearing American victory slogans or the face of George Washington, it is not safe to assume that it was made domestically. Americans generally considered the British wares to be better, so much so that the pottery made at Bennington, Vermont, during this time was often unmarked to allow it to be sold as British goods.

Despite having masqueraded as imported goods, Bennington is some of the best-known pottery to have been produced in New England. A number of kilns operated over the years at Bennington. The first was set up in 1785 by Captain John Norton and produced common red pottery and stoneware. Then the pottery works debuted a new creation called "yellow-ware," which was meant to imitate English creamware. In 1839, Norton brought his son-in-law, Christopher Fenton, into the business. Fenton was skilled in pottery making, and the firm began to expand its repertoire.

Various offshoots of the original firm appeared over the years, and as a result a number of fine wares have come to be associated with Bennington: flint enamel jugs in the form of a man; gray stoneware jugs; imitation Rockinghamware, which before firing is spattered with a brown, black, yellow, or olive green glaze to achieve a mottled appearance that closely resembles its namesake; and Parian ware, which is unglazed soft porcelain or bone china. Such products are today avidly collected, and some of the best examples are on display in museums, most notably the Metropolitan Museum of Art in New York.

Among the most collectible pottery is undoubtedly what is termed "art pottery." A major center for art pottery in New England was Chelsea, Massachusetts, where the Chelsea Ceramic Art Works thrived from 1872 to 1889. This pottery works produced red bisqueware, which were urn-shaped pieces with black backgrounds and red figures, reminiscent of ancient Greek vases. Headed by Hugh Robertson, who through much experimentation developed a red *sang de boeuf* glaze in imitation of the Chinese style, the company offered objects with a satin-like finish—not only in red but also apple green, mustard yellow and teal. The company changed its name to Chelsea Pottery U.S. in 1891 and was in business to 1896. The distinctive symbol 'CPUS,' which stands for "Chelsea Pottery U.S.," identifies works from this period.

A significant New England pottery center was Dedham, Massachusetts, which produced Dedham Pottery. This company was begun by Hugh Robertson. Products included "volcanic ware"—pieces fired ten or so times to create a mottling and striping of the paste glaze so that it resembled a volcanic eruption—and crackleware, molded tableware with borders decorated with repetitive patterns depicting rabbits and other animals. In the center of the plates were cracked lines resembling a broken egg. Dedham pottery also usually has telltale fingerprints on its underside, revealing where the potter held the plate while glazing it.

Shelburne Museum, Shelburne, Vermont

Another wonderful collectible is Paul Revere pottery. This Boston-based firm employed young immigrant women and operated from 1906 to 1942. Begun by a wealthy Boston woman, the firm was originally a club called the Saturday Evening Girls (S.E.G. is sometimes written on the pottery) that was organized to teach young women skills and keep them occupied. It eventually became a thriving business. The pottery the women created was affordable and imaginative: vases, children's dishes, and tiles with matte glazes finished in a variety of colors—yellow, blue, red, and maroon. Designs included nursery-rhyme themes and animals as well as flamboyant flowers—such as chrysanthemums, irises, and nasturtiums. Tiles usually depicted scenes of Boston life. These pieces are often signed with the artist's initials, and aside from the S.E.G. designation, might say "Bowl Shop," "Revere Pottery," or "P.R.P.," for Paul Revere Pottery.

NEW ENGLAND GARDENS

From the humble dooryard gardens of the
colonists to the cranberry bogs of Cape Cod,
New Englanders have always cultivated the
soil. The cool climate of New England poses a
challenge to gardeners: The growing season is
short and one has to contend with frosts and
extreme winters. But because of winter's
harshness, the mild months—when fruits,
flowers, and vegetables grow abundantly—
are appreciated all the more.

The region is rich in native edible plants—
such as the cranberry, blueberry, and many
wild herbs—yet the first New England settlers
industriously laid out gardens to supplement

the natural bounty. Although these early gardens were planted for utility rather than for beauty, they were characterized by a simple charm. Even today, gardeners in New England and elsewhere re-create the humble plots of the settlers—brimming with a variety of edible plants and enclosed by a picket fence—and many such gardens can be visited at historic New England homes.

For those with more elaborate tastes, the increasingly sophisticated New England gardens of succeeding centuries might be even more appealing. Eighteenth-century gardens were built on the previous era's design, yet with more fanciful touches such as benches, statues, and ponds. A visit to the homes and gardens of Newport, Rhode Island, is certainly in order to witness garden formality at its peak, at the end of the eighteenth and on into the nineteenth centuries.

While New England is rich in cultivated land, it is also a region of great natural beauty. Naturally scenic places such as Cape Cod and the Berkshires retain their wild, unstudied beauty. And in some places New Englanders have capitalized on nature's own designs. Wildflower and bog gardens are regional specialties, featuring native plants.

© George Livadaras/Envision

alls and fences are straight-forward methods of dividing gardens. The produce and cutting plots as well as the lawn are neatly separated by walls in a farm garden (page 110). The New England countryside is a natural garden tinged by a limitless palette (top). Adams House in Quincy, Massachusetts, was a working farm when the former president purchased it. Nearby the house, the old decorative flower gardens tended by Abigail Adams still survive (bottom).

W

113

© Paul E. Johnson/Decisive Moment

© Derek Fell

COLONIAL GARDENS

The history of Colonial gardens in New England begins not with the traditional image of the Colonial homestead, but with explorers traveling through the countryside, racing each other to claim land for their respective countries. In those early days, the explorers would quickly plant makeshift gardens to see them through the few months they would spend at a particular location.

The first Colonial New England garden on record was located in what is now Maine but in the early seventeenth century was known as New France. Samuel de Champlain planted the garden sometime around 1619 on an island in the St. Croix River. An account in his *Les Voyages* relates that de Champlain and his men returned a year after abandoning the garden and found it quite overgrown but were still able to put together a wonderful meal of lettuce, sorrel, and cabbage. De Champlain's sketches of the garden indicate a parterre style of very sophisticated arabesques directly derived from the European school of gardening. This plan was most likely an extreme exaggeration; explorers in a strange land would hardly have time to cultivate formal gardens, and vegetables can be harvested most easily when they are planted in straight rows. At around the same time that de Champlain planted his garden, the British explorer Captain John Smith also cultivated a thriving garden on a Maine island; it, too, was a garden of utility—a salad garden.

These itinerants' gardens, humble and artless as they no doubt were, demonstrate how vital gardening was to people roughing it in the wilderness of New England. A century would pass before anyone really had the leisure time to indulge in that craft known as ornamental gardening.

114

The Maria Mitchell Herb Garden

On blustery Nantucket, an island off of the coast of Massachusetts settled in 1659, the dooryard garden was an essential part of Colonial life. A larder and medicine cupboard well stocked with the garden's harvest was essential in seeing the hardy inhabitants through the cold winters. Looking much as it would have in the seventeenth and eighteenth centuries, the Maria Mitchell Herb Garden re-creates the straightforward yet elegant dooryard style of Colonial times. The garden is located close to a famous astronomical observatory erected as a tribute to the nineteenth-century pioneering woman and Nantucket resident Maria Mitchell —who among other things, discovered comets, was the first female professor in the United States, and toured major observatories around the globe in pursuit of her passion, the stars.

Although Mitchell lived in the nineteenth century, the Nantucket Maria Mitchell Association wanted to create an herb garden that would reflect traditional New England life. The garden's designer, Kitty Weeks, explains the simple yet effective structure of the garden, the same arrangement that would have benefited the seventeenth- and eighteenth-century family living in New England: "I have put the medicinal and dyeing herbs together in a bed along the side of the wall by the back door. And then all the culinary herbs are together on the right hand side, with a few decorative ones also added. There is a walk between them. Of course, all the herbs are close to the house, as it would have been in Colonial times."

Weeks describes the garden as a "living museum" because it so accurately represents the dooryard style. "This is a sampler of the different herbs you would have found if you walked into history," she says. As with most herb gardens, the best time to visit is June and July. In the late spring the roses and violets are out, followed by the lavender and dianthus. At summer's peak, chamomile, beebalm, calendula, and hollyhock all grace the garden. Generally speaking, herb gardens wind down at the end of August, so try to make your visit in the late spring or summer.

Of course, not all of more than sixty plants growing at the garden would necessarily have been grown in every colonist's garden. As Kitty Weeks points out, the housewife would have grown some plants in greater quantities than others. Popular culinary and household herbs would have been grown in large amounts. The medicinal plants masterwort and rue wouldn't have been used as frequently, although an all-purpose wonder drug like tansy would have been grown plentifully.

If you want to create your own dooryard garden, follow Kitty Weeks's example and consult the proper sources. Helpful, historically accurate books include Ann Leighton's *Early American Gardens: "For Meate or Medicine"*, Alice M. Coats's *Flowers and Their Histories*, and *Culpeper's Complete Herbal*, which was written in the seventeenth century but has been reprinted. Weeks stresses consulting several sources to come up with a well-rounded list of plants for your garden. As Weeks observes, separating the culinary from the medicinal and household herbs is important, since their uses are so different. A medicinal herb such as foxglove should only be enjoyed for its beauty. Although it truly does yield a heart medicine, this is no plant for the layperson to experiment with. Keep foxglove and other medicinal plants distinctly separated from your culinary herbs so that they're not accidentally plucked and tossed into a salad.

116

Pilgrim's Progress

Aside from the Native Americans, the Puritans were the first to plant for permanence in New England. The Pilgrims, who landed at Plymouth, New England, in 1620, were separatist Puritans not well-versed in the ways of the country. At first, they subsisted on what they foraged from the wild. Later, the settlers learned agricultural methods from the Native Americans, who also taught them how to cook and preserve the abundance of diverse native plants, such as maize and beans. William Bradford, governor of the Plymouth Plantation, saw fit to commit to paper what actually grew in the colonies' gardens, writing, "All sorts of roots and herbes in gardens grow."

The first gardens of the New England settlers were not elaborate or in any way imitative of sophisticated European styles. The emphasis was on low maintenance rather than design, on utility rather than beauty. And yet, sometimes the simplest of things are the most beautiful, because the result of their labors was the classic New England dooryard garden.

Colonial New England dooryard gardens were the woman's domain. She chose the plants to use for every conceivable household purpose, simultaneously playing the roles of family doctor and cook. Puritan pioneer women relied on the designs provided in a few popular horticultural books of the day to lay out their gardens. The first book written specifically on American kitchen gardening was *A treatise on Gardening,* by John Randolph, Jr., published in 1780. Before this, the colonists had turned to the British for advice, specifically John Parkinson's *Paradisi in Sole Paradisus Terrestris* and Leonard Meager's *English Gardener.* Parkinson

Picket fences are classic aspects of New England garden design. A weathered picket fence surrounds a vegetable plot containing natural wood stakes. The majority of New Englanders prefer to cultivate simply designed gardens such as this one.

117

*T*hese plants are in raised boxes to ensure proper soil drainage (this page). It looks as though this charming house in Mystic Seaport, Connecticut, is about to be overgrown by its luscious garden (page 119).

© Derek Fell

recommended the "four-square forme," equally divided into squares, with herbs and flowers growing in the quadrants. The most salient quality of this garden was its usefulness. Meager also advocated simplicity, writing, "Tread out your beds handsome and straight by a line."

By and large, the New England dooryard garden was rectangular. The house sat on one edge of the rectangle, and a road on the other. The dooryard garden had to be located close by the abode, so that the woman of the house could easily harvest plant materials for various uses, whether it was to add subtle flavor and color to a salad with

violet leaves, sweeten the air in the house with lavender cotton, or dress a wound with woundwort. It was invariably a compact space surrounded by a whitewashed picket fence, and the industrious Puritan woman divided beds into neat, geometrical sections with paths running between them. She usually planted the culinary herbs on one side of the garden and medicinal and household herbs on the other. Many of the plants were grown from seeds the colonists had brought with them from England. But the Puritan housewife had to allow herself some indulgences in her strange new surroundings, and so she grew a few

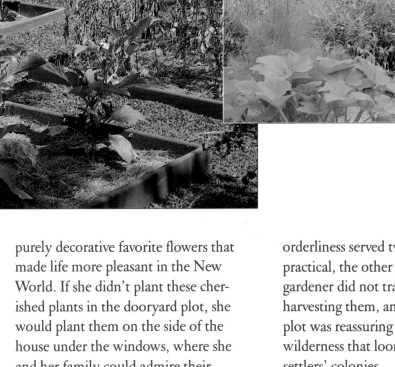

© Derek Fell

purely decorative favorite flowers that made life more pleasant in the New World. If she didn't plant these cherished plants in the dooryard plot, she would plant them on the side of the house under the windows, where she and her family could admire their beauty and enjoy the sweet scents that wafted into the house.

Garden historians have likened these early gardens to the cottage gardens of the settlers' ancestors. But while the dooryard style is as unpretentious as the cottage garden—in which plants serving a variety of useful purposes are grown in beautiful profusion side by side—it is also more orderly. This orderliness served two purposes, one practical, the other psychological: The gardener did not trample plants when harvesting them, and the neatness of plot was reassuring amid the vast wilderness that loomed beyond the settlers' colonies.

As time went on, the designs of dooryard gardens became more intricate. The geometry of their design became more elaborate, and circles, triangles, and even knot shapes were used in addition to the simple, humble square. No matter how sophisticated the dooryard garden became, however, the gardens were still located next to the house.

*Calendula blos-
soms (this page,
top) were used in salads
and as dyes; the plant
was also employed as a
wound salve. Peony was
grown strictly as an
ornamental flower (this
page, bottom). Beebalm
was used in making
a medicinal tea (page
121). Flower beds are
surrounded by stones in
this New England gar-
den (page 122-123).*

Dooryard Garden Plant List

There were many plants cultivated in the Colonial period, so
the following list is a selection of
those used, with some of their
original uses given alongside
them.

Many of the plants are herbs
and have several uses, both
culinary and medicinal. The
plants in the decorative category
were cultivated for their garden
beauty and for use in drying and
flower arrangements, tussie-
mussies, and wreaths. You might
use this list as a starting point for
creating your own New England
dooryard garden.

© Derek Fell

© Derek Fell

Decorative

candytuft (*Iberis* species)

canterbury bells (*Campanula medium*)

foxglove (*Digitalis purpurea*)

hollyhock (*Althaea rosea*)

lily of the valley (*Convallaria majalis*)

love-in-a-mist (*Nigella damascena*)

peony (*Paeonia officinalis*)

Venus's looking-glass (*Specularia
perfoliata*)

white lily (*Lilium candidum*)

Culinary

angelica (*Angelica archangelica*), candied
stem

calendula (*Calendula officinalis*),
blossoms in salads

caraway (*Carum carvi*), seeds baked in
bread

chamomile (*Anthemis nobilis*), meat
preservative, tea

chives (*Allium schoenoprasum*), soups
and salads

clary sage (*Salvia sclarea*), omelets

clove pink (*Dianthus caryophyllus*),
syrups

dill (*Antheum graveolons*), sauces

hops (*Humulus lupulus*), beer flavoring

lettuces (*Lactuca* species), salads, juice
induces sleep

parsley (*Petroselinum hortense*), broths,
spider repellent

rose (*Rosa* species), petal jams, wines,
and vinegars

salad burnet (*Poterium sanguisorba*),
salad herbs, drink flavoring

salad rocket (*Erica sativa*), salads, freckle
cure

sorrel (*Rumex acetosa*), relishes, sauces

violets (*Viola* species), blossoms in
salads

© Derek Fell

Household and Medicinal

beebalm (*Monarda didyma*), medicinal tea

catnip (*Nepeta cataria*), medicinal tea

costmary (*Chrysanthemum balsamita*), potpourris

elecampane (*Inula helenium*), lung problems

lady's bedstraw (*Galium verum*), mattress filler

lavender (*Lavandula* species), potpourri and soap

madder (*Rubia tinctorium*), dye plant

masterwort (*Astrantia major*), root used as tonic

rue (*Ruta graveolons*), poultice, poison antidote

shepherd's purse (*Capsella bursa-pastoris*), head-wound ointment

spearmint (*Mentha spicata*), nerve strengthener

tansy (*Tanacetum vulgare*), embalming herb, insect repellent

valerian (*Valeriana officinalis*), sedative

yarrow (*Achillea millefolium*), insect repellent

BEEBALM

During the period following the Boston Tea Party of 1773, Yankee ingenuity was hard at work inventing substitutes for the traditional, heavily taxed China tea. To assuage their teatime cravings, the colonists turned to the plants that grew in their gardens and in the wild. One of the most popular plants for this purpose was beebalm, Monarda didyma, *a plant with brilliant red flowers. It was introduced to New Englanders by the Native Americans, who used it for tea, thus inspiring another common name for the plant, Oswego tea. The tea made from the dried leaves was thought to relieve stomach and bronchial maladies. Sage-leaf and berry-leaf teas were also popular substitutes for traditional black tea. Among the berry varieties used were strawberry, currant, and blackberry leaves. Raspberry leaves were especially popular, inspiring the grandiose name Hyperion Tea, named for the ancient Greek sun god. Although you could probably purchase some of these tea blends today, it's more fun to cultivate the plants in your home "tea garden" and dry the leaves to create your own blends of New England–style teas.*

122

NEW ENGLAND STATES

STATE	NICKNAME	ORIGIN
Connecticut	Constitution State, Nutmeg State	From Mohican and Algonquin words meaning, "long river place."
Maine	Pine Tree State	Named for an ancient French province
Massachusetts	Bay State	A Native American tribal name meaning, "large hill place."
New Hampshire	Granite State	Named after a county in England.
Rhode Island	Ocean State	Exact origin unknown. Possibly named after the Mediterranean Island, Rhodes
Vermont	Green Mountain State	From the French words, *vert* (green) and *mont* (mountain).

FLOWER	BIRD	TREE
Mountain Laurel	American Robin	White Oak
White Pine Cone and Tassel	Chickadee	Eastern White Pine
Mayflower	Chickadee	American Elm
Purple Lilac	Purple Finch	White Birch
Violet	Rhode Island Red	Red Maple
Red Clover	Hermit Thrush	Sugar Maple

The Age of Formality

Formal gardens have a long tradition in New England. Rhode Island has its share of these exquisite gardens, as evidenced by these topiary animals (page 127) and this perfectly groomed flower and hedge garden (page 128-129).

As the eighteenth century drew to a close, more sophisticated gardens debuted in New England on country estates. A movement toward greater formality in garden design took hold. People were finally realizing wealth through American industry, and the nouveau riche wanted to flaunt it. What better place to display wealth and social prestige than in their gardens.

Such traditionally European garden touches as statues, garden follies, parterres (gardens using plants, walkways, and terraces to emphasize formalized geometric patterns along the ground), ornamental ponds and fountains, stylized flower beds, and ornate seating were introduced to the formerly humble New England garden. The middle class began to add such fussy touches as crushed shells between paths to their gardens. People even had the leisure time to cultivate that ultimate luxury, the grassy lawn.

In 1838, the Boston Public Garden was opened in a romantic setting of diversified plantings punctuated by a lagoon. The Arnold Arboretum debuted in 1872 in Boston. This garden was designed by Frederick Law Olmstead, famous for his ability to balance plantings with vistas and wide open spaces, and included many rare exotic plants and flowering shrubs in a meticulously landscaped setting.

The gardens of the mansions of Newport, Rhode Island, demonstrate the height of Victorian and turn-of-the-century garden extravagance. The city was founded in 1639 by a small group of colonists who had left Boston behind, but in the mid-nineteenth century became a summer haven for wealthy, industrial magnates. Many extravagant gardens, not to mention homes, were undertaken there. In the mid-nineteenth century, Chateau-sur-Mer, a Victorian mansion with grounds meticulously landscaped with exotic plantings and a great lawn, was built. A perhaps even more trumped-up lawn was designed at the Elms, an eighteenth-century adaptation of a French chateau. Also adding to the rarified Old World atmosphere were sunken gardens and a terrace garden populated with marble and bronze statues. The turn-of-the-century home Rose Cliff—replete with flower urns modeled after those at Versailles, rose gardens, fountains, and statues—is one such example.

In Rhode Island on Upper Narragansett Bay in 1880, Thomas Brayton began practicing the unusual Old World art of topiary—a method for creating shapes with shrubbery through the use of meticulous pruning and wire. Working with his Portuguese gardener, Joseph Carreiro, who was skilled in such garden arts, Brayton conceived of a garden in which animals fashioned from privet and boxwood roamed. The duck, camel, bear, swan, horse, and donkey are among the animals populating the garden, which is still open today and is maintained in the most meticulous fashion. Brayton died in 1939, but he passed the property along to his daughter, Alice, who developed the formal gardens further.

Such Old World style flourishes in New England unquestionably resulted in beautiful gardens. But another movement in garden design was also brewing. It began on the other side of the Atlantic, but soon took over America.

GARDENS

GARDENS

*T*he meticulously sculpted menagerie at Green Animals in Rhode Island (pages 128-129) is one of the world's foremost topiary collections. The formal gardens are also punctuated by geometric forms. Low-growing, feathery-leaved ferns are among the most ancient of plants and take on a variety of shapes throughout New England (page 130, bottom). The region is also rich with streams and unspoiled woodlands (page 130, top).

130

© Jeremy Barnard/Decisive Moment

© Jeremy Barnard/Decisive Moment

Natural New England Gardens

In the late nineteenth century in England, William Robinson espoused his philosophy of letting a garden grow in a natural setting. He encapsulated his thoughts in the famous book *The Wild Garden*, which opposed the studied formality of Victorian gardens featuring carpet bedding—flowers planted in elaborate patterns resembling Oriental rugs—and other fancy touches. By the turn of the century, this fervor had caught on and a new recognition of the importance of native plantings emerged. In America, the fervor also spread, and as the twentieth century progressed, people came to appreciate the wild space.

Such nineteenth-century American writers as Henry David Thoreau helped set the stage in New England for an appreciation of its natural charms. Thoreau celebrated the natural beauty of the countryside in his famous *Walden Pond* as well as in other essays. And in the twentieth century, Robert Frost's haunting, wise poems such as "Mending Wall" and "After Apple-Picking" captured the essence of rural New England living.

As a direct result of this heightened awareness of New England's wild beauty, much of the land has been left unspoiled, and today New England's most famous and beautiful garden is the natural environment. To experience New England as a garden, the nature lover can visit many beautiful sites in each state. In Massachusetts, there is the Cape Cod National Seashore, where dunes and wild cranberries grow and also offer natural examples of the bog garden; the Allyn Cox Reservation in Essex, where you can take a lovely nature walk complete with identifying labels for many of the plants; and the Walden Pond Reservation in Concord. In Rhode Island, Napatree Point near Watch Hill is a scenic spot, and the Mohegan Bluffs on Block Island lure visitors with their charms. In Connecticut, Hubbard Park in Meriden contains a nature trail among undulating hills, and Topsmead State Forest in Litchfield offers both open meadows and forestland. Maine's Kennebunk area, Acadia National Park, Mount Desert Island, and Pemaquid area are all natural gardens. Damariscove Island is owned by the Nature Conservancy and has an interesting combination of native and introduced flora. In Vermont, Rhododendron State Park in Fitzwilliam attracts visitors to view the spectacular rhododendrons growing in wild profusion, at their peak in July, and the Long Trail traverses the stunning Green Mountains. New Hampshire's White Mountains, part of the Appalachian Trail system, are also worth visiting to experience their beauty; think of the trail as a great garden path. And, of course, fall foliage throughout the entire New England region is the most spectacular garden display of all.

Garden in the Woods

Will Curtis was one of the premier pioneers of the natural-garden philosophy in New England. He was a dedicated naturalist, following in the footsteps of the work of naturalists such as William Robinson in England and John Muir in America. Curtis had been trained at Cornell University as a landscape architect, but preferred to go by the title "landscapist" or "landscape designer," these being more descriptive of working with plants, not buildings.

In 1931, he acquired a forty-five-acre tract of land in Framingham, Massachusetts. Curtis was particularly taken with this land because it had been shaped by the retreating glaciers of the Ice Age, which produced a remarkably varied landscape of streams, pools, and even gently undulating hills. He felt that the land so embodied the range of natural environments, not only in New England but also across North America, that he purchased it with the dream of turning it into a wonderful naturalistic garden that would conserve and show off the beauty of indigenous flora. He wanted to tamper with the land as little as possible to create his natural garden.

Curtis teamed up with another horticultural enthusiast, Howard Stiles, and the two began to transform the tract.

Three years later, Garden in the Woods debuted, with the co-founders' proclamation that they wanted to "curb the wholesale destruction of our most beautiful natives." The garden was entrusted to the New England Wildflower Society in 1965. Since then, the society has remained true to the co-founders' original intent: to promote the conservation of native American plants.

David Longland, executive director of the Garden in the Woods, stresses this philosophy: "We're here to protect the native species. We do this through the medium of the naturalistic garden." By making people aware of the beauty of the native plants, says Longland, the garden prompts the question: These things are beautiful; are they not worth conserving?

The handiwork of Curtis and Stiles is still spectacular. Among the unique environments they created are the Woodland Groves, Lily Pond, Rockeries, Sunny Bog, Pine Barren, Meadow, and Western Scree. Perhaps of most interest to New England enthusiasts is Laurel Bend, a collection of drought-tolerant wildflowers of the natural New England landscape.

Some people might scoff at the idea of wildflowers, preferring showier cultivated hybrids like roses. Longland and the Wildflower Society believe these native plants have garden value because of the "powerful beauty in the subtlety." Says Longland, "When Will Curtis established the garden, he was trying to promote native plants as being just as garden-worthy as the European plants people were growing in the 1930s. He thought North American plants were undervalued."

Longland points to the purple pitcher plant and pink lady's slipper as some of the very beautiful plants indigenous to New England that visitors to the garden can enjoy. The latter is "protected by an archaic Massachusetts law. Some people try to dig them up and put them in gardens, but they're killing the plant." Should you wish to create a native wildflower garden, make sure that you are not gathering endangered species from the wild and that your site is compatible with the growing conditions of the plant, as Will Curtis did.

Says Longland, "Curtis also believed, and we uphold his philosophy, that the highest of art forms is expressed in nature." At the Garden in the Woods, the landscape is like a canvas transformed dramatically several times a year. Spring brings hepatica, trailing arbutus, yellow lady's slippers, and trillium; summer dazzles with pitcher plants, turk's cap lilies, and blazing stars; late summer is alive with cardinal flowers and turtleheads; and the meadow in autumn sparkles with gentians, asters, and goldenrod.

Of course, New England is famous for its fall foliage. And the Garden in the Woods is also a place of pilgrimage for this display. Longland says that at this garden there are "more different kinds of foliage than anywhere else in New England. A lot of people will drive to Vermont for flaming sugar maples, which are beautiful. But we have 1,500 different taxa, and a lot of these take on special visual interest. There's no place else where you can see so many different plants turning colors. The peak time is the third week of October, but the change starts in the beginning of September and builds. It's my favorite time of the year here—it's a tapestry."

Formal gardens with great, open lawns and carefully arranged, symmetrically laid-out flower borders are designed to dazzle the garden visitor with their awesome sense of order. The Garden in the Woods does the opposite. Longland calls it "a small-scale intimate garden that you walk *into*. It sets the mood from the beginning with a sense of peace and privacy."

Autumn foliage officially signals the end of the brief New England summer and heralds the beginning of the long winter (page 132, top). At the Arnold Arboretum, autumn brings a multicolored carpet of leaves (page 132, bottom).

133

*T*he cinnamon fern is so named because of its brownish fronds (this page, top). Lady's slipper is a member of the orchid family (this page, bottom). Cardinal flower can be seen growing wild in Cape Cod (page 135, top). Delicate jack-in-the-pulpit flowers blossom from mid-May to June (page 135, bottom).

© Derek Fell

© Derek Fell

134

The New England Bog Garden

Bog gardens contain delicate orchid family members and lacy ferns and are quite stunning as a natural-looking accent in the yard. They should only be planted in sites with moist, rich acid soil. You'll also need a sunken area of ground that will be inundated by water part of the year. If this isn't possible, construct a minibog using a container. Sink it about a foot into the ground, and plant it with a variety of interesting species. The following plants are all bog-loving plants that are native to New England. If you live in an area where these plants will not thrive, consult specialized texts to find relatives that will grow in your area. Some New England bog gardens that you can visit are the Mount Monadnock Alpine Bog in Monadnock State Park in Joffrey, New Hampshire; the Wayne Bog, in Wayne, Maine; and the natural bogs of the Cape Cod National Seashore.

Selected Planting List

cardinal flower (*Lobelia cardinalis*)

cinnamon fern (*Osmunda cinnamonea*)

interrupted fern (*Osmunda claytoniana*)

jack-in-the-pulpit (*Arisaema triphyllum*)

maidenhair fern (*Adiantum pedatum*)

marsh fern (*Dryopteris thelypteris*)

netted chain fern (*Woodwardia areolata*)

nodding lady's tresses (*Spiranthes cernua*)

pickerel weed (*Pontederia cordata*)

purple pitcher plant (*Sarracenia purpurea*)

royal fern (*Osmunda regalis*)

turk's cap lily (*Lilium superbum*)

yellow lady's slipper (*Cypripedium calceolus*)

© Derek Fell

© Derek Fell

THE APPALACHIAN TRAIL

The Appalachian Trail, which is 2,023 miles long and runs from Georgia through Mount Katahdin, Maine, was the brainchild of the New England writer Benton Mackaye. Mackaye conceived the idea in 1921. By 1925, the Appalachian Trail Conference had formed—various groups of hikers banded together to unite footpaths into one long trail. By 1937, the trail was completed. But its completion didn't interest only hikers. An Appalachian Trail enthusiast who was locally famous in her day was Mrs. Fred Hutchinson, who lived in the Berkshires in a house beside the trail. Mrs. Hutchinson greatly admired those hikers who braved long distances of the trail, and for more than fifty years, she made it her business to cater to tired, hungry trekkers' needs when they passed by her house. In the early part of this century, trail hikers were newsworthy, and Mrs. Hutchinson would scan papers, and listen to the local gossip for word of their impending arrival. After ascertaining that a hiker was in the vicinity, she would dispatch scouts to greet him or her with an invitation of food and a shower. While the hiker was eating, she would read aloud from Robert Frost, the quintessential New England poet. Mrs. Hutchinson died in 1975. She was eighty-nine years old.

Appendix

Antique Fairs/Crafts Fairs/ Food Festivals

March

Maine Maple Sunday
Maine Department of Agriculture
Bureau of Agricultural Marketing
State House Station 28
Augusta, ME 04333

August

The Maine Festival of the Arts, Inc.
29 Forest Avenue
Portland, ME 04101

September

Common Ground Country Fair
Maine Organic Farmers and
Gardeners Association
P.O. Box 2176
Augusta, ME 04330

Throughout the Year

Bean-in-the-Hole Suppers
Flanders' Bean-Hole-Bean Company
P.O. Box 313
Epsom, NH 03234

Furniture and Interiors

Brookline Village Antiques
18 Harvard Street
Brookline, MA 02146
turn-of-the-century lighting and
eighteenth- and nineteenth-century
American furnishings

Dovetail Woodworks
99 Prescott Street
Worcester, MA 01605
fine woodworking

Fort Point Cabinetmakers
368 Congress Street
Boston, MA 02210
craftsman cooperative producing
eighteenth-century reproductions

Hilary House
86 Chestnut Street
Boston, MA 02108
eighteenth- and nineteenth-century
American furnishings and
collectibles

Marcia & Bea Antiques
1 Lincoln Street
New Highlands, MA 02161
furniture and collectibles

Period Furniture Hardware Company
123 Charles Street
Boston, MA 02114
reproduction brass hardware

Shreve, Crump & Low
330 Boylston Street
Boston, MA 02116
furniture and collectibles

Yield House
Dept. 1000
North Conway, NH 03680
selection of classic New England
designs—such as ladderback chairs
and Shaker designs, some in kit
form

Gardens and Nature Trails

American Indian Archaeological Institute
Curtis Road
Washington, CT 06793
wild native plants used for medicine, dyes, and food

Arnold Arboretum of Harvard University
125 Arborway
Jamaica Plains, MA 02130
broad range of plants—from exotics to flowering shrubs and vines—grouped by families on grounds designed by Frederick Law Olmstead

Berkshire Garden Center
Routes 102 and 183
Stockbridge, MA 02162
garden with culinary and medicinal herbs; perennial border

Canterbury Shaker Village
288 Shaker Road
Canterbury, NH 03224
Shaker museum with herb garden

Caprilands Herb Farm
534 Silver Street
Coventry, CT 06238
plants and seeds, including numerous Allium species, lavenders, mints, oreganos, upright and prostrate rosemaries, culinary and creeping thymes, angelica, catnip, lovage, hyssop, bee balm, sweet rocket, yarrows; also has extensive selection of herbal crafts, such as scented wreaths, rosebud balls, and lavender sachets

Garden in the Woods
New England Wildflower Society
Hemenway Road
Framingham, MA 01701
native plants on 42 acres

Green Animals Topiary Garden
380 Cory's Lane
Portsmouth, RI 02781
famed sculpted shrub animal garden

Hancock Shaker Village
P.O. Box 898
Pittsfield, MA 01202
Shaker herb garden

Heritage Plantation of Sandwich
Grove and Pine Streets
Sandwich, MA 02563
rhododendrons and native plants

Maria Mitchell Science Center
2 Vestal Street
Nantucket, MA 02554
herb and wildflower gardens

New Alchemy Institute
237 Hatchville Road
East Falmouth, MA 02536
research gardens open to public

Old Sturbridge Village
One Old Sturbridge Road
Sturbridge, MA 01566
period herb and flower gardens

Old Slater Mill Museum, Fiber and Dye Garden
P.O. Box 727
Pawtucket, RI 02862
small but interesting fiber and dye garden

Plimouth Plantation
Route 3A
Plymouth, MA 02360
seventeenth-century-style village; kitchen gardens with herbs

Vermont Wildflower Farm
P.O. Box 5, Route 7
Charlotte, VT 05445
wildflowers

Historic Houses, Museums, and Exhibits

Maine

Washburn-Norlands Living Center
RD 2, Box 3395
Livermore Falls, ME 04254

Sarah Orne Jewett House
5 Portland Street
South Berwick, ME 03908
Georgian-style home with nineteenth-century interiors

Sayward-Wheeler House
Barrell Lane
York Harbor, ME 03911
Colonial-era home containing Queen Anne and Chippendale collections

Massachusetts

John Gardner-Pinigree House
Essex Institute Museum
132 Essex Street
Salem, MA 01970
contains work of Salem master builder Samuel McIntire

Harrison Gray Otis House
141 Cambridge Street
Boston, MA 02114
Federal-style home designed by Charles Bulfinch

Hancock Shaker Village
P.O. Box 898
Pittsfield, MA 01202
Shaker crafts, homes, lifestyle

House of Seven Gables
54 Turner Street
Salem, MA 01970
famous seventeenth-century house

Jeremiah Lee Mansion
P.O. Box 1048
Marblehead, MA 01945
Georgian period home

Nantucket Historical Association
P.O. Box 1016
Nantucket, MA 02554
maintains eleven properties, including Quaker meeting house and seventeenth- and eighteenth-century homes

New Bedford Glass Museum
50 North Second Street
New Bedford, MA 02740
glassware housed in Federal-Style mansion

North Bennet Street School
39 North Bennet Street
Boston, MA 02113
New England's oldest trade school features periodic exhibits of traditional furniture making and handcrafting

Chesterwood
A National Trust for Historic Preservation Property
Stockbridge, MA 02162
art museum and historic home of sculptor Daniel Chesterwood

John Whipple House
53 South Main Street
Ipswich, MA 01938
seventeenth-century home with period furnishings

New Hampshire

Gilman Garrison House
12 Water Street
Exeter, NH 03833
originally a garrison home, now remodeled in Georgian style

Pierce Manse
P.O. Box 425
Concord, NH 03302
Victorian-era home with authentic furnishings; lilac and ornamental shrubbery gardens

Vermont

The Bennington Museum
West Main Street
Bennington, VT 05201
Bennington pottery collection, as well as Vermont glass, chests, and other American pieces

Park McCullough House
P.O. Box 366
North Bennington, VT 05257
Victorian-era New England home; also features Colonial-style garden

Sandwich Glass Museum
129 Main Street
Sandwich, MA 02563
exhibits of famed Sandwich glass

Shelburne Farms
Shelburne, VT 05482
nineteenth-century agricultural estate

Shelburne Museum
Route 7
Shelburne, VT 05482
period buildings and exhibits; also features garden with culinary, fragrance, and dye herbs

138

Mail-Order Foods

Cabot Creamery
P.O. Box 128
Cabot, VT 05647
cheese

Crowley Cheese
Healdville, VT 05758
cheese

Gray's Grist Mill
P.O. Box 422
Adamsville, RI 02801
stone-ground flint corn meal,
johnnycake meal

Lawrence's Smoke House
Rt. 30
RR #1, Box 28
Newfane, VT 05345
corn-cob smoked ham

Kenyon Corn Meal Company
Usquepaugh, RI 02892
stone-ground clamcake mix,
johnnycake meal

L.L. Bean
Route 1
Freeport, ME 04033
assorted foods from New England

Maine Seaweed Company
Box 57
Steuben, ME 04680
edible seaweed and other sea
vegetables

Rawon Brook Farm
New Marlboro Road
Monterey, MA 01245
goat's milk cheese

New Penny Farm
Route 2, Box 45
Presque Isle, ME 04769
Maine potatoes

Shelburne Farms
Bay Road
Shelburne, VT 05482
cheese, maple syrup, Vermont
products

'Stache Foods
P.O. Box 705
Damariscotta, ME 04543
maple barbecue sauce

The Store
26 Mill Street
Orono, ME 04473
assorted foods from Maine

United Society of Shakers
Attn: Herbs
Sabbathday Lake, ME 04274
herbs and herbal teas

The Vermont Country Store
Mail Order Office
P.O. Box 1108
Manchester Center, VT 05255-1088
Vermont common crackers

Auction Houses and Antique Dealers

Richard A. Bourne Co., Inc.
P.O. Box 401
Hyannisport, MA 02647
auction house

Robert W. Skinner, Inc.
Route 117
Bolton, MA 01740
auction house

Bibliography

American Heritage magazine editors. *A Guide to America's Greatest Historic Places.* New York: American Heritage, 1987.

Bishop, Robert, Judith Reiter Weissman, Michael McManus, and Henry Niemann. *The Knopf Collectors' Guides to American Antiques: Folk Art.* New York: Alfred A. Knopf, Inc., 1983.

Bishop, Robert, and Patricia Coblentz. *A Gallery of American Weathervanes and Whirligigs.* New York: E.P. Dutton, Inc., 1981.

Black, Naomi, and Mark Smith. *The American Mail-Order Gourmet: The Catalog of Hundreds of Hard-to-find Delectable Delights.* Philadelphia: Running Press Book Publishers, 1986.

Blanchan, Neltje. *The American Flower Garden.* New York: Doubleday, Page & Co., 1913.

Butler, Joseph T. Illustrations by Ray Skibinski. *Field Guide to American Antique Furniture.* New York: Henry Holt, 1985.

Carpenter, Ralph E., Jr. *The Fifty Best Historic American Houses.* New York: E.P. Dutton & Co., 1955.

Coats, Alice. *Flowers and Their Histories.* New York: Pitman Press, 1956.

Deerfield Parish Guild. *The Pocumtuc Housewife: A Guide to Domestic Cookery as it is Practiced in the Connecticut Valley [by Several Ladies].* Deerfield, MA: The Deerfield Parish Guild of the First Church of Deerfield, 1985 (reprint of 1897 edition from 1805 sources).

Earle, Alice Morse. *Home Life in Colonial Days.* Stockbridge, MA: Berkshire Traveller Press, 1974 (reprint of 1898 edition).

Earle, Alice Morse. *Old-Time Gardens.* New York: Macmillan, 1901.

Eaton, Allen. *Handicrafts of New England.* New York: Harper and Bros., 1949.

Fairbanks, Jonathan L., and Bidwell Bates, Elizabeth. *American Furniture: 1620 to the Present.* New York: Richard Marek Publishers, 1981.

Favretti, Rudy J., and Joy. *For Every House a Garden: A Guide for Reproducing Period Gardens.* Chester, Conn.: The Pequot Press, 1977.

Fitzgerald, Ken. *Weathervanes and Whirligigs.* New York: Clarkson N. Potter, Inc., 1967.

Flayderman, E. Norman. *Scrimshaw and Scrimshanders.* New Milford, CT: N. Flayderman and Co., Inc., 1973.

Gunst, Kathy, and John Randolph. *The Great New England Food Guide.* New York: Arbor House/William Morrow and Company, Inc., 1988.

Kaye, Myrna. *Fake, Fraud, or Genuine?: Identifying Authentic American Furniture.* Boston: New York Graphic Society, 1987.

Kimball, Fiske. *Domestic Architecture of the American Colonies and of the Early Republic.* New York: Dover, 1966.

140

Kirk, John T. *Early American Furniture: How to Recognize, Evaluate, Buy and Care for the Most Beautiful Pieces—High Style, Country, Primitive & Rustic.* New York: Alfred A. Knopf, 1970.

Leighton, Ann. *Early American Gardens: 'For Meate or Medicine.'* Boston: Houghton Mifflin, 1970.

Lord, Priscilla S., and Daniel J. Foley. *The Folk Arts and Crafts of New England.* Radnor, PA: Chilton Book Co., 1965.

Morrison, Hugh. *Early American Architecture From the First Colonial Settlements to the National Record.* New York: Oxford University Press, 1952.

National Gallery of Art, ed. *An American Sampler: Folk Art from the Shelburne Museum.* Washington, DC: National Gallery of Art, 1987.

Rifkind, Carole. *A Field Guide to American Architecture.* New York: New American Library, 1980.

Rodriguez Roque, Oswaldo. *American Furniture at Chipstone.* Madison, Wis.: The University of Wisconsin Press, 1984.

Root, Waverly. *Food: An Authoritative and Visual History and Dictionary of the Foods of the World.* New York: Simon and Schuster, 1980.

Schwartz, Marvin D. *American Furniture of the Colonial Period.* New York: Metropolitan Museum of Art, n.d.

Shurtleff, Harold R. *The Log Cabin Myth: A Study of the Early Dwellings of the English Colonists in North America.* Gloucester, Mass.: Peter Smith, 1967.

Simmons, Amelia. *The First American Cookbook: A Facsimile of "American Cookery," 1796 by Amelia Simmons.* New York: Dover Publications, Inc., 1984.

Teleki, Gloria Roth. *Collecting Traditional American Basketry.* New York: E.P. Dutton, Inc., 1979.

Whiffen, Marcus. *American Architecture Since 1780: A Guide to the Styles.* Cambridge, Mass.: M.I.T. Press, 1969.

Yeager, Carole. *Yankee Folk Crafts.* Dublin, NH: Yankee Books, 1988.

Index

142

143